VIETNAM INC.
Philip Jones Griffiths

VIETNAM INC.
Philip Jones Griffiths

COLLIER BOOKS, New York, New York
Collier-Macmillan Ltd., London

This book is dedicated to the memory of all those photographers who died in Indochina and in particular to that of Larry Burrows, Henri Huet, Kyoichi Sawada, and Keisaburo Shimamoto.

The Macmillan Company
866 Third Avenue, New York, N.Y. 10022
Collier-Macmillan Canada Ltd., Toronto, Ontario

Vietnam Inc. is also published in a hardcover
edition by The Macmillan Company.

Library of Congress Catalog Card Number: 73-167932

First Collier Books Edition 1971

Printed in the United States of America

I am indebted to my colleagues at MAGNUM for their generous assistance—P.J.G.

Glossary

A book about the Vietnam war is bound, unfortunately, to need an extensive glossary to guide the reader through the fog of Orwellian "newspeak" that the United States employs in an attempt to disguise its activities. This one is as short as possible, commensurate with elucidating the text. In addition, for the purpose of acquainting the reader with the gravity of the lexical war, there is reproduced below the "Proper Terminology Determination" guide — entitled, as one might guess, "Let's Say It Right!" — which is issued to the military information officers who write press releases for journalists.

The use of the word Vietcong (VC) throughout this book is of no political significance. It happens to be the word most in common usage. It is not meant to imply that all VC are communist — on the contrary, they are primarily nationalists. Neither is any attempt made, within the book, to subdivide the People's Liberation Armed Forces into the much-favored groups like "guerrilla," "main force VC," or even "NVA" (North Vietnamese Army). The latter is particularly meaningless since all Vietnamese (with perhaps the exception of those North Vietnamese who are, curiously enough, in control of the U.S.-backed military regime in the South) will insist that they are one people.

PROPER TERMINOLOGY DETERMINATION

INCORRECT TERMS	CORRECT TERMS
South Vietnam	Republic of Vietnam (RVN)
Democratic Republic of Vietnam	North Vietnam
South Vietnamese Army	Army of the Republic of Vietnam (ARVN)
People's Army of North Vietnam	North Vietnamese Army (NVA)
People's Liberation Army	Vietcong (or if appropriate, North Vietnamese Army — NVA)
Ruff-puff	Regional Forces Popular Forces (RF/PF)
Mercenary	Civilian Irregular Defense Group (CIDG) soldier or volunteer
VC tax collectors	VC extortionists
Search and destroy	Search and clear
Body count	Enemy deaths or EN killed
U.S. troop withdrawal	Redeployment (or replacement)
Hamburger Hill	Hill 937
Troops used to bait the enemy	Never to be used
Deserter or defector (VC)	Rallier or returnee
Free-fire zone	Pre-cleared firing area
Retreat	Tactical redeployment
Ambushed	Engaged the enemy on all sides
Booby trap	Automatic ambush
"Hearts and minds of the people"	"Develop community spirit" or equivalent descriptive phrases
Vietnamization	Favorable term for the process of turning over our efforts to the Vietnamese people
Five o'clock follies	MACV daily briefings (or daily press briefings)

AMERICAL DIVISION — notorious Army division also known as the Amerikill, Atrocical, and Americalley Division

APC — Armoured Personnel Carrier, a lightweight tank without gun turret

C-RATIONS — tinned food issued to soldiers in the field

CHIEU HOI — defector from the VC

"CONTESTED" AREA — a place where Americans get shot at

DISTRICT SENIOR ADVISOR — the American who advises the Vietnamese District Chief

FRIENDSHIP KITS — gifts given to Vietnamese in the hope of winning their friendship

GVN — Government of South Vietnam

IR8 "MIRACLE" RICE — U.S.-developed strain of high-yield rice that Vietnamese regard in about the same way a French gourmet would frozen TV dinners

M16 — standard-issue U.S. field rifle based on the outlawed dum-dum bullet

MACV — U.S. Military Assistance Command in South Vietnam

"MOTIVATED" — inspired

PX — Post Exchange, or supermarkets for the military

PSY-OPS — Psychological Operations

REFUGEE — a person that has been forced to leave his home

RELOCATION — forced removal

RESTRUCTURING — moving people and burning their homes

SAM MISSILES — Soviet surface-to-air missiles

USAID — United States Agency for International Development

USO — United Services Organization, which provides recreational facilities for soldiers in the cities and bases in Vietnam

VNC — Vietnamese civilian

"VOTING WITH THEIR FEET" — what Americans say of Vietnamese who they consider to have voluntarily left areas of VC control

Introduction

In Vietnam can now be seen the opening round of the last big fight, the conflict between East and West — that ultimate conflict which will determine the shape of mankind's future. The values of Western democracy are being pitted against those of China. This war in Vietnam is the beginning of the war with China (for Vietnam is ideologically a part of China) and the war is qualitatively different from all others because it is being fought not for sea routes or land, but for the minds of men.

America is trying to sell a doctrine to the Vietnamese. For a hundred years it tried to sell the same thing to China. America's overwhelming interest in China was in obtaining for itself the qualification of maturity that would be bestowed on the nation responsible for bringing China into the open after 3,000 years of obscurity. But despite the enticements and the Coca-Cola, China turned and bit the hand that was tempting it toward "civilization." America never forgave China, perhaps because it could never understand how any country could *choose* communism. So it put the rejection of Americanism down to a Russian plot or a collective madness of the Chinese people, while never questioning the desirability of the doctrine it was exporting. This same misplaced confidence in the universal goodness of American values was to prompt their imposition on the Vietnamese.

The opportunity arose when, in order to keep Europe strong against the latest common enemy, Russia, the United States decided to mollify France by helping it in that most un-American activity, a colonialist war. When France was forced to quit, America stayed on, using the excuse of "containing" that "expansionist delinquent," China, thereby creating the American dependency of South Vietnam. France was an embarassment: its hands were tarnished as a colonial power; it had come to Vietnam to loot. America came to take nothing, only to give. And all it asked in return was that the Vietnamese accept its values, norms, morals, and beliefs — in short, its total ideology.

For ten years, from 1954 to 1964, America tried the "soft sell." Over the years, in the face of increasing failure, the selling became harder. The salesmen grew impatient and any resistance was attributed to a communist plot (which was, after all, the only logical reason for anyone to reject a product of such self-evident excellence). And it became all right to kill off anyone sick enough to prefer the other brand, communism. By 1965 sales resistance was so great the Marines had to be sent in to carry out the hard sell, followed by an additional 2,000,000 military men. The sell became tougher still — but so did the resistance. More drastic measures had to be taken. Vietnam had to be "restructured" to allow better "sales penetration" and more people had to be killed, until finally the ultimate absurdity was reached: the people were being killed to be "saved" from the different flavor of the other brand.

This view of America's involvement in Vietnam is, admittedly, at variance with the commonly held one that sees the whole venture as a simple case of the American military-industrial complex practicing genocide on the Vietnamese. That America somehow planned Vietnam as the grand spectacle to intimidate would-be revolutionaries throughout the third world by showing them how ruthlessly they would be suppressed requires a belief in the omnipotence of U.S. foreign policy. And such a belief can only be held by those who have not seen the salesmen of American policy in action.

This book will, I hope, reveal that the events in Vietnam occurred because of the absence of the restraining influence of consummate wisdom. For the overwhelming impression afforded by Americans in Vietnam is one of stupidity rather than evil, an observation accentuated by comparison with the Vietnamese.

I contend that Vietnam is the goldfish bowl where the values of Americans and Vietnamese can be observed, studied, and because of their contrasting nature, more easily appraised. I maintain that the reason America became involved in Vietnam and the reason for its failing so dramatically there is because of fundamental deficiencies within the American system.

This book is not, however, intended to be a list of the tactics which failed, compiled for the purpose of overcoming the deficiencies and ensuring success next time. The American miscalculations made in Vietnam are overshadowed by and stem from the folly of the original view that deemed it possible for a society like America's to impose itself on that of the Vietnamese. This view was based on an ignorance that later frustrated progress and prompted recourse to the asset America has in abundance — the tools of destruction. And so, hand in hand with increasing failures, more and more death was rained down on the Vietnamese people. Despite the moral censure of mankind, and to the eternal shame of the American people, the killing continues today.

The Vietnamese Village

RICE is traditionally threshed by walking a buffalo over it. This costs nothing and is a pleasant way to spend an evening.

The Vietnamese are a rice-growing people. For two thousand years their adeptness at pursuing this perennial task has been sustained by their belief in a harmony between man and nature. This belief, born of Buddhism, structured by Confucianism, and mystified by Taoism, sees every man, every thought, every action as significant and interrelated within a universal order. It transcends Western religious dogmas: it is a collective acceptance of values recognized by all for their self-evident virtue.

The environment, their world, is the paddy field, and their horizons are delineated by the borders of these flat rice lands. For a thousand years they grew rice in the Red River Delta, near the Chinese border, before beginning their "march south" along the fertile coastal strip into the present-day delta region of South Vietnam. They moved along by cultivating rice lands and seeding them with villages — a slow expansion southward which the indigenous Hindu kingdom of Champa, for all its military might, was unable to stop. For a thousand years they have been moving over a distance of a thousand miles and there is no reason to

think that they have stopped: a hundred years ago, France thwarted their designs on Cambodia; now America has made them feasible.

The secret of their strength lies in the nature of their society. The foundation of their society is the village. Set amid the sea of rice fields, villages rise like identical islands, surrounded by sheer cliffs of bamboo. Inside live those who tend the rice, in great proximity to one another (every precious bit of land is needed for rice-growing), but within a well-organized whole. Traditionally, each village is autonomous. The state used to be represented by the Emperor, who had little temporal power: "The authority of the Emperor stops at the gate of the village," as the old saying goes. Within this decentralized state, power resided in the hands of the people in the villages. While each village was a self-contained unit, independent, self-sufficient, and relying on no one, it was bound to each and every other village as a partner in the common task of growing rice. Harmony as the supreme virtue — and being part of that harmony — was the motivating force, enabling the villagers to accept

toil in the fields. Rites and rituals gave meaning to the work far beyond simply providing food to eat. In the fields were buried one's ancestors whose spirit passed through the soil into the rice, so that eating it became the ritual by which one inherited one's ancestors' souls.

Within the village structure, the individual gained his peace of mind through the passive security afforded by the public knowledge of his place in society. The role he was to play, the attitudes he must adopt, his relationships toward everything — these were all predetermined by tradition. To transgress these norms would earn the castigation of his fellow villagers; to fulfill them would reinforce his place within the integrated whole of the social unit. Inside this rigidly compartmentalized structure, there was little room for individuality in the Western sense of the word. In fact, the tensions and feelings of claustrophobia induced by these highly public living conditions were prevented from surfacing — as this would bring disharmony to village life — by means of careful adherence to the Confucian rules that governed social behavior. The idea of moderation at all times — which meant always maintaining an even temper as proof that the individual was just and honorable — was central. Any outbursts of anger were condemned, not by chastisement but derision: any show of force was regarded as proof of inferiority. The self-expression encouraged today in the West to counter the dire consequences of bottling up one's feelings appears incongruous when applied to the Vietnamese. Generations of suppressing emotions by means of thoughtful introspection have endowed them with powers of perception which class them as intellectual giants.

It is the Vietnamese psyche, the supreme achievement of the village system, that is the bastion of the Vietnamese nation. From the very beginning, no outsider could claim to have conquered Vietnam until the last village had fallen. This has never happened because no attacker has ever had enough soldiers to conquer every fortified village from the disadvantageous position of exposed paddy fields. An invader could assert that a village had been taken, but eventually even this claim would turn out to be hollow. For, with nothing much to loot (the village economy was simple and accumulated no wealth), it was only a question of time before the invaders left. Those foolhardy enough to try to dominate the people by "winning the hearts and minds" — as the current U.S. jargon puts it — left soon after, for the Vietnamese have a way of reducing such attempts to futile charades. For over a thousand years, from 111 B.C. to 938 A.D., the Chinese tried this and failed. What the Vietnamese learned in that period has enabled them to throw off, in turn, the Mongolians, the French, and, barring the event of a fit of nuclear pique by the Strategic Air Command, the Americans. They know that to survive one pretends to acquiesce; one collaborates without imparting useful information; one offers no resistance when surrender is tactically sound: in fact, one subjugates all personal passions — like hate, contempt, fury — for the higher goal of persuading the invader to leave. Persuasion was always the key tactic. Rarely were the Vietnamese strong enough to expel the invader by force, and this is certainly the case with the Americans. Once the Marines had landed in 1965 on the beaches of Vietnam, the efforts of all Vietnamese, except for a few who stood to gain financially, have been to persuade the United States to withdraw its troops. Previously, American aid could be tolerated — there is a long tradition of exploiting one's enemy's resources — but half

CHILDREN of Chothom, the village in Kien Hoa province where the NLF originated.

a million troops tearing apart the very fabric of one's society was another matter.

For what American policy has attempted to do is to obliterate the village as a social unit. This, ostensibly, is in order to deny cover to the guerilla, but, in reality, the purpose is to reconstruct Vietnamese society in the image of that of the United States. John Vann, widely regarded as one of the most articulate and experienced Americans in Vietnam, recognized this when he wrote some years ago that a battle was taking place to revolutionize Vietnam and it was the duty of Americans to ensure that the conversion was to Western democracy, not Communism. The fact ignored in this statement is that the Vietnamese have already had their revolution: anything America is trying to achieve is being done against the will of the people. I have never met any Vietnamese who could relate to America's claim to be liberating him from his traditional past.

How, then, does one account for what appear to be the visible signs of America's success in changing the people? How does one account for all the GVN flags loyally flying outside many villagers' homes, which make the local advisor so proud and happy? The answer is that their allegiance is ruled by expedience: they would hang out ten foot hand-woven tapestries of the face of Spiro Agnew if it ensured freedom from bombing. That this is so should surprise no one: the Vietnamese national emblem depicts a cluster of bamboo, which the people revere as a symbol of strength, and about which they have a saying: "The bamboo bends under the wind and survives, while the pine stands erect and is hurled down."

EVERY HOME has a thick slab of hardwood, used as table, bed, and air-raid shelter.

RICE is the staple diet. But it is more than food to the Vietnamese — it is their purpose for existing. A symbiosis exists between the society's religious beliefs (its moral values) and its task of growing rice. To a Vietnamese, each meal has some of the significance that eating Communion bread has for a Catholic. Nowadays, American rice has to be sent to Vietnam to feed those driven from the land. The people hate it; they try to sell it for pig food to get money to buy what Vietnamese rice is available. (It is, of course, perfectly wholesome — but so is canned dog food, which no American would eat however many vitamins it contained.) With as much as half (according to one report) of the arable land rendered barren by U.S. defoliation, plus the destruction of dikes and also the "free-fire" zone designation which prevents the people from working it, Americans now place great importance on the introduction of new "miracle" rice strains to increase production on the remaining land. In this way it is hoped that the people will have less need to return to the land from which they were forcibly removed.

THE OLDEST and the most venerated man in the village with his great-grandchildren. Torn posters describing the life of Buddha adorn the w

e childrens' mother left the village to "work" for the Americans. Being just as beautiful as their mother, her daughters are destined to follow.

THE PEASANTS spend most of their lives in their rice fields and when they die they are buried there. Thus, they believe their spirits will pass through the soil into the rice when they die, so that their souls will be inherited by their descendants when the rice is eaten. As a result of the war, there now exist graveyards of the Western type, for it is not always possible to return the bodies of those killed in battles to their homes. Nevertheless, in the case of the Vietcong graveyard (opposite), where slain fighters of the front lie buried beneath headstones with five-pointed stars on them, villagers make sure the warriors' souls will not ''wander through eternity'' by feeding their cows (later to be eaten) on the grass that grows over the graves.

"Why We're There"

A CIA-ORGANIZED demonstration of "spontaneous" anger against those favoring a negotiated settlement of the war.

In the center of downtown Saigon is a restaurant called Brodard's. It is the only really American-looking eating house around — plastic tables, lots of bright lights, mirrors galore, arctic air-conditioning, a loud jukebox, and huge picture windows. Apprehensive American customers, trying to translate "Bouche Lorraine" while listening to Edith Piaf, consider the place far too French. It was here I talked to my first American in Vietnam. He leaned over from the next table saying, "Excuse me, sir, can you tell me what's the white powder in this jar?" When I realized he wasn't joking, I explained that it was salt; that salt cellars do not work because of the humidity and so it is put in open jars. He "much appreciated" my telling him this and with relief said now he understood why the waiter had not brought any and why he'd had to eat his french fries without, although he'd asked for some twice. At this point he noticed my accent. "Say, you're English! I'd like to shake you by the hand, sir! I really like the English. Feel kind of close to them. I'm proud that we Americans are now doing what your great country did for three hundred years. That great Queen Elizabeth of yours going out to bring civilization to

Africa and India. Well, now I guess it's our turn, seeing how England's kind of given up. Yes, sir! America's proud to take up where you left off!" By the time he'd finished speaking, he was standing, his eyes glazed. Amazed at his behavior, I tried to amuse him by saying that as a Welshman I'd been on the receiving end of English expansionism and so could not be expected to share his sentiments. He ignored this and kept repeating how privileged he was to meet someone whose ancestors had "shown the light to India." He left — with the waiters having a laugh about him as he stumbled out into the street.

At the time, his view of America's interest in Vietnam was too farfetched to be taken seriously, but over the next few years I was to hear it on many occasions. Every time an American criticized a Vietnamese, the criticism was based on a self-righteous sense of natural superiority derived from unquestioning belief in an American monopoly of all higher morality. A belief that prompted President Johnson, in his inaugural address, to say: "The American covenant called on us to help show the way for the liberation of man. That is still our goal. . . . If American lives must end, and American treas-

ure be spilled, in countries we barely know, that is the price that change has demanded of conviction." For the most part, this conviction remains unexpressed. It is implicit in sayings like "We are here to help the Vietnamese help themselves," which have become common currency among Americans, and are considered truthful enunciations of admirable objectives (in much the same way as the advertised wetness and wildness of Seven Up). What the above saying really means is that America is giving assistance to those Vietnamese who make a show of aspiring (preferably spontaneously) to the foreign way of life being imposed on them. The conviction is inherent in another overworked adage: "We are here to ensure freedom for the Vietnamese to choose the kind of government they want," which is as implausible as Bell Telephone saying it believes everyone should have the freedom to choose which 'phone company to patronize. The meaning is, therefore, that the Vietnamese are free to choose provided they make the "right" choice and accept the American alternative. This saying is also the ultimate rationale of those involved in the military effort in Vietnam. Thus, to the soldier the situation is ex-

24

plained as follows: "The freedom-loving Vietnamese are being prevented from leading a quiet life by a lot of communists streaming down the Ho Chi Minh trail trying to take over the country by force. Under such circumstances, it is reasonable that America should go to the help of a country being so attacked and anyone who assumes we are there for an ulterior motive is wrong — we're there to give the Vietnamese the opportunity to decide for themselves." This account was given to me by a disillusioned GI who was confused by the conflicting realities of what he had been told and what he'd seen in Vietnam and who admitted that he wished he'd asked the briefer whether this freedom of choice GI's were dying for extended to that of the Vietnamese to choose communism. The answer would probably have been, "You must be joking!" The requirement of the American position is that South Vietnam adopt a new belief — and that belief is the doctrine of free-enterprise capitalistic democracy.

To many Americans, the most puzzling aspect of their task is the lack of "motivation" shown by the Vietnamese. Traveling around the provinces, one heard the same exasperated pleas from participants in the "WHAM" program (Winning Hearts And Minds!), as from those advisors to the Hamlet Animal Husbandry Coordinating Committee with their vision of a Vietnam content under a sea of rutting non-Communist pigs: "I've told them, the American people will give them the cement, the lumber, the tin roofing to build the sties and it will import the piglets (because Vietnamese pigs are too dirty — their stomachs hang in the mud as they have weak spines, you know) but godammit, I've told them, they've got to build it for themselves. Otherwise they won't think of it as theirs!"

Always, the pressure was to "help" and to "give" and the only thing asked in return was for whatever was offered to be accepted. For, if it was not, refusals might necessitate taking a tougher line and anything resembling firmness would smack of that word which every USAID worker detested more than all others — colonialism. To be described as colonialist was felt to be so unjust because America was obviously not there to take as France had been. Unfortunately, it was believed — not surprisingly by a property-fixated society — that the Vietnamese would give their hearts and minds to America far more readily than they had given their rubber to France.

The Vietnamese have never understood America's involvement in their country. For the most part, they have gone along with the Americans. There was no reason not to. Nothing much was asked in return — stick up a government flag outside your house, attend a few meetings without laughing while some foreign idiot told you what you'd already learned about pigs from your father when you were six years old, and, most important and easy, appear grateful. When dollars float down from the sky, who stops to ask questions? Paradoxically, by 1970 some of them were surrounded by an air of what was almost panic as the U.S. troop withdrawals began to get underway. One student complained that he could not possibly be expected to comprehend why the Americans were leaving when he still hadn't discovered why they had come in the first place!

But over the years many explanations have been attempted. A girl explained how, before she had left her village, a school friend tried to get her to join the Front in driving out the Americans. When she argued that the Americans didn't seem too bad, her friend gave her the Vietcong line which was . . . near Hanoi was a mountain made of gold . . . the French had failed to find it and now the Americans were trying . . . it was her duty to kill them, to stop them stealing what belonged to the Vietnamese people. While this interpretation of the behavior of the American Army may seem ludicrous to the reader, it is far more acceptable to a peasant (average wage, one hundred piasters a day) than would be trying to explain away a "search and destroy" operation in which five hundred soldiers, whose lives are collectively insured for six billion two hundred and fifty million piasters, arrive in helicopters costing two billion five hundred million piasters to search an area as if they're *looking for something;* pay lots attention

to *high ground;* never pass a *cave* without searching it; and even die in large numbers in attempting to get onto *mountain* tops.

In fact, the main thrust of NLF propaganda is aimed at the chauvinism of the Vietnamese. Rallying calls are made "to drive out the Americans trying to take over Vietnam"—an observation so real to the Vietnamese that discussion over the reasons is superfluous.

One bizarre explanation, most certainly started by observant Vietnamese fisherman rather than by the propaganda machine in Hanoi, was that Americans were in Vietnam to take away the sand from the beaches. The Vietnamese, noticing the enthusiasm with which Americans lie on beaches assume they derive some great unknown benefit from sand for which they're even prepared to endure having their skins burned and darkened (in Vietnam a dark skin confers social inferiority, so no sane Vietnamese peasant would consider lying on a beach). Since, up and down the coast of Vietnam, Americans can be seen filling sacks with sand and taking them away in trucks, this seems proof enough. But perhaps someone explained that they use the sand-filled bags to make bunkers. "Ah!" someone else would point out, "what about the big ships that come to take the sand away?" It is true. Huge quantities of sand are shipped abroad to make glass because Vietnamese sand is almost pure silica. However, it all goes to Japan.

The attempts continue to provide an explanation. The latest one by Vietnamese intellectuals came recently with the announcement that oil had been found in Vietnam. But this too proved untenable when it was realized that the oil had been found long after the U.S. build-up.

U.S. COMBAT TROOPS ARRIVE, outnumbering the enemy 3 to 1 and possessing the most sophisticated military hardware; the job seemed

THE VIETNAMESE PEASANT reacts to the arrival of foreign soldiers in the traditional way — with a smile. Putting the foreigner at ease increases his confidence, making its collapse all the more dramatic. This policy has always worked in the past: too weak to drive out the invaders by force, the Vietnamese have always managed to make them "decide to leave." At first, it is the children who show their hostility, until they too realize they have more to gain by a show of friendship. In return for allowing themselves to be fondled, children can expect a steady flow of candy, cigarettes, and C-rations. The "cuter" the child, the more it can get. A pretty daughter can feed a family for days, producing a stockpile of gifts which a parent guards while she returns empty-handed for more. Such behavior is interpreted by GI's as confirmation of the love they were promised as "liberators of the Vietnamese people."

SOLDIERS never marched, they hunted "Cong" by helicopter or even on elephants (beflagged, for U.S. pilots shoot all elephants as VC

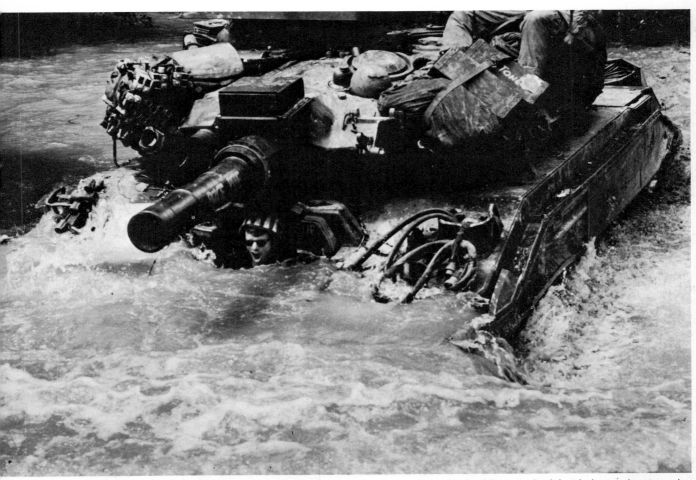

ER was the great concern. Some GI's refill their canteens during a monsoon downpour (top) while a tank sinks during a river crossing.

ANXIOUS MOTHER (opposite) looks on as a Marine embraces her child. Most GI's search desperately for sincere friendship during their stay in Vietnam. They discover they cannot find any or buy any, even from the whores. Often it is a Vietnamese dog that becomes their best friend. It is estimated that more dogs than wives have been taken back to the United States by returning GI's.

Children (right) never cease to be fascinated by the hair on GIs' bodies. "Gorilla" is one of the expressions most commonly used by Vietnamese when referring to Americans.

"CAR WASHES" (below) are brothels where GI drivers stop to get their trucks hosed down. Wherever Americans congregate, scores of girls are always waiting to sell them souvenirs, beers (stolen from the PX), marijuana, heroin, and themselves.

LIMITS OF FRIENDSHIP. A Marine introduces a peasant girl to king-sized filter-tips. Of all the U.S. forces in Vietnam, it was the Marines that approached "Civic Action" with gusto. From their barrage of handouts, one discovers that, in the month of January 1967 alone, they gave away to the Vietnamese 101,535 pounds of food, 4,810 pounds of soap, 14,662 books and magazines, 106 pounds of candy, 1,215 toys, and 1 midwifery kit. In the same month they gave the Vietnamese 530 free haircuts

CAR PURCHASING during combat. Salesmen used to follow GI's into the field to make a sale "so that the boys will have a real reason for wanting to get home in one piece." Today they find it safer to have the GI choose his car's trim and upholstery by mail order.

ARVN SOLDIER enters battle armed with toothbrush and playmate. Ten-year-old ARVN (top left), a "little tiger" feted for killing two "Vietcong women cadre" the day before (his teacher and mother, it was rumored). ARVN colonel and his U.S. adviser (top right).

ARVN SOLDIERS off to loot and rape in Cambodia. Many Americans interpreted their enthusiasm as proof of a new-found aggressiv

CAPTURED VIETCONG. It is difficult to avoid the conclusion that the effect of American involvement in Vietnam has been to differentiate the most admirable Vietnamese from the most deplorable. The values that the Vietnamese regard highly are possessed almost exclusively by the Vietcong. These values are nowhere better set down in writing than in the national poem *Kim Van Kieu,* which is a veritable handbook on the Vietnamese psyche, yet is virtually unread by Americans. In it is chronicled the life of the heroine, Thuy Kieu, with whom the Vietnamese, as a nation, identify. In her adventures, mostly sad, can be seen the moral blueprint which all Vietnamese live by. These values are either unknown to or trampled over by Americans, who are anxious to replace them with those for a new society built up of individuals "motivated" by personal greed. The ARVN are earmarked to be part of this new society. These soldiers, unable or unwilling to resist the easy life afforded by the ARVN (compared with fighting for the Vietcong), harbor a deep resentment toward their "masters," the Americans, as foreigners who are trying to divide Vietnam.

For the captured Vietcong shown here there is no equivocation. They are firmly set in the honorable tradition of sacrificing one's life for one's country. The woman (opposite) was the sole survivor of a communications squad caught in the open. Wounded in the spine, she was forced to crouch all day with her hands tied behind her back before being taken off by helicopter. When reproached, a U.S. officer replied, "What's the hurry? When the GVN boys have interrogated her, she'll only be raped and killed anyway."

As Thuy Kieu declared in the poem:
It is better that I should sacrifice myself alone,
It matters little if a flower falls if the tree can keep its leaves green.

HE ENEMY. His lack of equipment is a constant source of wonder to the GI's. Surrounded, this Vietcong "defected," in the best Maoist tradition

Caught in the wires of an "automatic ambush," he produced a Chieu Hoi (safe conduct) pass to classify himself as a "rallier" to the GVN side

WOUNDED VIETCONG . . . GI's often show a compassion for the enemy that springs from admiration of their dedication and bravery. This VC had a three-day-old stomach wound. He'd picked up his intestines and put them in an enamel cooking bowl (borrowed from a surprised farmer's wife) and strapped it around his middle. As he was being carried to the headquarters company for interrogation, he indicated he was thirsty. "OK, him VC, him drink dirty water," said the Vietnamese interpreter, pointing to the brown paddy-field. With real anger a GI told him to keep quiet, then mumbled, "Any soldier who can fight for three days with his insides out can drink from my canteen any time!"

The Communication Gap

In the 1963 edition of the *Encyclopaedia Britannica,* under the heading of "Linguistics," there appears the following passage by G. L. Tragar,

". . . When translation is between two languages that are structurally similar and whose speakers are culturally related as a whole, as between English and French, it is possible for the skilled translator to convey real equivalences of meaning in all or nearly all cases.... But if the languages in question are dissimilar structurally, as are English and Vietnamese, and the cultures as a whole are different, as are those of American and Vietnam, then the problem of translation becomes very great; one really has to have full micro-linguistic analyses of both languages and extensive general cultural knowledge and analysis."

It now seems ironic that Vietnamese and English should have been chosen as examples and a pity that the message went unheard by a nation so inundated by encyclopaedias.

For it is rare to find in Vietnam an American who doesn't believe that communication with the Vietnamese is as good as his phrase book. Yet the best phrase book is valueless. Even being able to speak the language does not really help. Ultimately, Americans would have to understand Vietnamese mentality. Thus there exists a group which is totally cut off by the language barrier from the realities of situations it needs to comprehend in order to accomplish its dubious task of "saving the Vietnamese." Seeing Americans in action in Vietnam, being exploited by a few Vietnamese for political or financial gain and hated by the rest — while courting the few and attempting to kill the rest, one is torn between a gratitude that the ignorance that they are being duped precludes their taking more drastic measures and a natural resentment at seeing anyone being exploited. But even this conflict of feelings is muted by seeing the almost masochistic delight Americans exhibit while being taken for a ride and the unequalled expertise with which the Vietnamese drive them round in circles. (This exploitation and manipulation by the Vietnamese is not confined to Americans. I remember in 1967 meeting the puzzled *Pravda* correspondent in Phnom Penh. "I don't know why we let them get away with it!" he moaned. Just back from North Vietnam, he was amazed at the way in which, at Haiphong harbor, skippers of Russian ships were being persuaded to hand over their cargoes of S.A.M. missiles without the accompanying "technicians" to supervise the installation. With despair he added, "they load them on their trucks, simply hand us a receipt and that's the last we ever see of them.")

For, in all their circumventions, it is the way the Vietnamese have mobilized language as the finest weapon for achieving objectives that constitutes their greatest triumph. It is the first line of defense employed to deny information to opponents. It allows them to preserve an inner privacy amid a most public pounding by an alien force. And it acts as a cohesive force uniting the Vietnamese people at a time when their external world is being fragmented.

The Vietnamese language, like the Vietnamese people, originated in China. It is a tonal language, and, despite the impressive fact that one third of the world's population speaks tonal languages, it is not a very effective way of communicating. Vietnamese is based on monosyllabic words, utilizing a very restricted range of sounds which are expanded by means of tones to produce enough words for a working language. While it can be argued that this unfavorable view of the Vietnamese language stems from a Westerner's lack of familiarity with the undoubtedly admirable poetic nuances afforded by a tonal language, and that the Vietnamese, and especially the Chinese, could not be expected to have stuck with an inefficient language for many millennia, the fact is that the most common word in the Vietnamese language is "Err?" which means "Would you repeat what you said?"

Observations of everyday Vietnamese speech show that much of what the Vietnamese say to each other is not understood the first time — phrases are often repeated, sometimes two or three times. Modern noise levels might be partly to blame — it must be difficult to separate the preglottalized imploded sound from that of the retroflex affricate against a background roar of airconditioners or motorcycles. However, little more than a mild cold is sufficient to make communication very hazardous, and possibly one of the riskiest situations to be in is that of a patient in a Vietnamese operating theater, where, because of the facemasks worn, instructions given by the surgeon to his assistants have a good chance of not being understood. For this reason Vietnamese doctors rarely wear masks except when there is an American "advisor" around who has to be kept happy.

When a Vietnamese says something, his necessary preoccupation with the tones of individual words he's speaking nullifies any overall tone he might be expected to impart to the sentence. So a question, quite likely, would not have a rising tone, though possibly the answer might. Often a GI will ask one Vietnamese why two others are arguing so heatedly and feel cheated when told truthfully that they are amicably discussing, say, a wedding they attended. Couple this with an almost complete absence of gesticulations (on the ground that any necessity to provide an adjunct to one's words betrays a lack of confidence in their value), the result is that the only way to comprehend spoken Vietnamese is to have a finely tuned ear for tonal nuances comparable to that of the best piano tuner around.

Turning to the written language in the hope of finding a clearer delineation of words, one reels back from a text seemingly designed for maximum indecipherability. Vietnamese was traditionally written in the form of Chinese characters until these officially gave place in 1910 to a romanized script, which was codified in 1650 by a French priest. He set about translating Vietnamese sounds into French words. He expanded the French alphabet by borrowing a few letters from the Portuguese and Italian alphabets and adding diacritics galore. Consequently, in modern Vietnamese, letters from the Roman alphabet end up as twelve vowels, seventeen consonants and nineteen double consonants! This number is still not nearly enough to match the spoken language, however, because the six tones must also be indicated. This calls for more diacritics, which means that the text looks as though it is trying to revert to its original character form. A road sign, for instance, has far more in common with Japanese finger painting than words. While this may be considered charming, it can hardly be regarded as satisfactory for the day when Vietnam will have fast throughways.

The difficulty a foreigner has in passing from written to spoken Vietnamese has enabled the language to be used as the greatest defense. In practice, it means that a Vietnamese never has to understand what is being asked of him and that he is free to do anything contradictory on the ground that he has not understood the speaker. The plausibility of this defense rests on the fact that it is considered reasonable to misunderstand an American trying to talk Vietnamese. After all, since the Vietnamese themselves don't understand each other half of the time, how can they be expected to understand when a foreigner speaks their language? Couple American eagerness always to give to the Vietnamese the benefit of any doubt with an inherent naïveté and situations will occur like the one in which the ARVN captain, having been entrusted with five tons of rice for feeding some refugees, sold it on the black market and explained later through an interpreter that he had understood his American counterpart to have said it was to be given away for pig food. The American, proud of his few words of Vietnamese, then entered into a friendly discussion with his interpreter to try to discover where he'd slipped up with pronunciation, while the rice was forgotten (not to mention the hungry refugees).

It is naturally assumed that any Vietnamese is allowed to "not hear" or to misunderstand when addressed in English. Those whose command of English seems adequate when soliciting help or handouts, are in no way singled out even

if, upon being asked for something in return, their knowledge of English suddenly dries up. One of the facts that the Vietnamese are ever anxious to implant in the minds of foreigners is that they are a somewhat delicate, easily offended people, for whom to "lose face" is disastrous, and that therefore the foreigner should expect a Vietnamese always to agree, rather than to admit he doesn't understand. Needless to say, this excuse is most frequently invoked, as in the familiar situation where the Ameri-

can has asked the Vietnamese if the gun is loaded. The Vietnamese shakes his head to indicate he hasn't understood the question. The American takes this to mean that the gun is empty, but, to be certain, he gets the Vietnamese to agree that he has understood. Because he does not want to lose face, the Vietnamese does agree to having understood what was asked, and the American shoots himself through the foot. This explanation is taken as perfectly valid even if the Vietnamese wanted to see the American shoot himself. The result of this double standard is to afford the Vietnamese a total anarchy. For the most part, no one can understand them and they never have to understand anyone who is saying something they prefer to ignore.

To the keen American — who is not tone deaf and who is not discouraged about learning a language in which "Hello" and "Good-bye" are the same word, "black" is six different words depending on what it's describing, and the words for "yes" and "no" don't exist — there is a disappointment in store. For, despite all the encouragement offered by the professional welcomers-of-Americans-to-speak-Vietnamese (because "we really appreciate your honoring us by condescending to take interest in our

humble mother tongue, Mr. Mighty Dollar"), the fact is that Vietnamese hate foreigners who can speak their language. It is true that to give the opposite impression they pretend to show great pleasure when a foreigner manages a few words, but once his fluency reaches a certain point they feel threatened and uneasy. Ultimately, however, the real drawback to learning Vietnamese is that, as the man indicated in the encyclopaedia, fluency in the language doesn't confer communicability. The explanation for this lies

in an understanding of the nature of the traditional wholeness of Vietnamese society laid down according to Taoist and Confucian principles. These principles treat of man's participation in the universal order of things and clearly state the attitudes that each person should adopt toward all else so that everything — each action, deed, thought, utterance — is interrelated and interdependent. Nothing exists in isolation, everything is part of some other part that produces ultimately the totality of all the parts which is the universe itself. In this light, the language can be seen as a product of Confucian thought (whose primary function is to serve its political and social needs rather than to be concerned with anything as simple as communication).

Thus, the way one addresses a Vietnamese is more important than anything one may have to say to him. That there are no words for "yes" or "no" may seem ludicrous, but to a Vietnamese it would be ill-mannered to ask a question that would call for such an abrupt answer. And to answer a question like this would be insulting because it would imply that the questioner was too ignorant to know the correct answer. An abrupt answer or an insulting question is a transgression of the code of behavior embodied in the Confucian ethic.

To expect foreigners to be able to tune into this complexly structured existence, even when afforded every encouragement, is to be highly optimistic, especially in the case of the Americans whose alienation as a group from the Vietnamese is extreme; but, when the society as a whole is actively using every means possible to prevent its happening, the expectation is wildly unrealistic.

So, what the previous American administration should have asked itself is whether or not to become involved in revolutionizing (and simultaneously being exploited by) a people with whom it could not communicate: whether or not America should attempt to win the hearts and minds of a people who never reveal their desires and aspirations: whether or not it would be feasible to cooperate with a people who have a language that is impossible to speak and difficult to read even with the aid of a dictionary or phrase book, when, if one were to persist and succeed in learning the language, despite the resistance of the Vietnamese, communication would still be impossible without actually mentally becoming Vietnamese. To put it another way, was it fair to send American boys to a country where they have *twenty-five* different ways of pronouncing the word "Ma"?

WAR IN THE COUNTRYSIDE. Inability to find the enemy led to feelings of frustration. These U.S. 9th Division troops rarely "made con

GENERAL KINNARD of the 1st. Cav. proposed, "It occurred to me that perhaps we would be able to identify the guerrilla — a farmer by day and a fighter by night — by the dark circles under his eyes." It is not known how many people died because they yawned. **50**

PAGES 51 - 54 ARE MISSING

More recently, in keeping with efforts to automate the killing, enlarged ''people-sniffers'' slung under helicopters have been used. A ''positive'' reading is intercepted by a second, heavily armed helicopter that follows and automatically lets off a barrage of fire at the indicated position. In this way, no human decisions have to be made: a pair of helicopters skim over the countryside, the second raining death whenever the first detects molecules of amino-acid breakdown products, whether from buffalo, Vietcong, or children taking a short cut to school.

CORDING to the official U.S. Army handbook on Vietnam: ''. . . to win over the peasants, the Vietcong used terror and coercion while the vernment sought to extend effectively its educational, health and social welfare programs. The GI's who assumed the above to be true soned that peasants who still chose to live in VC-controlled areas and resisted being ''saved'' must therefore be crazy and so deserved to die.

MOTHER AND CHILD, shortly before being killed. A unit of the American Division operating in Quang Ngai Province six months before My Lai. The resentment was already there: this woman's husband, together with the other men left in the village, had been killed a few moments earlier because he was hiding in a tunnel. After blowing up all tunnels and bunkers where people could take refuge, GI's withdrew and called in artillery fire on the defenseless inhabitants.

INTERROGATING THE WOUNDED, and (opposite page) men of
the "Tropic Lightning," the 25th Infantry Division, leave their
"visiting cards" — torn-off shoulder patches depicting the division's emblem, a bolt of lightning — stuffed in the mouths of
people they kill. A platoon from the 1st Cavalry (below) kills still
another civilian (posthumously elevated to the rank of VC like all
the rest). The platoon, accompanied by an intelligence officer,
was heading for some caves where, according to a VC defector
who had been promised his life in exchange for the information,
his colleagues were hiding. Considering themselves to be walking
into a certain trap, most members of the platoon were very nervous. On seeing the first farmer, everyone opened up and missed.
One GI from Kansas cursed, "My Pa'd uv tanned my hide for
missing a shot like that." The next farmer was not so lucky: soon
he lay dying among the ripening rice in the corner of the paddy
field, the back of his skull blown away. He was still somehow con-
scious, making a whimpering sound and trying to squeeze his
eyes more tightly shut, while the officer kept on trying to question
him. He never spoke and died with the fingers of his left hand
clenching his testicles so tightly they could not be undone. "Got
him in the balls, knew I'd hit him!" cried the boy from Kansas
until someone took him to one side and explained that they do
that to relieve the pain elsewhere. As the body was turned over,
the right arm, which had been submerged until then, was revealed. It had no hand — it had previously been amputated above
the wrist. "I know I seen him before," said the officer's assistant.
"We checked him out yesterday. He's VNC (the classification for
innocent Vietnamese civilian)." "No! That one yesterday had his
left hand off," insisted the officer, looking guilty as the water of
the paddy field reddened.

HUMAN SKULLS were a favorite souvenir among the soldiers and their officers. The commander of this unit, Colonel (now Brigadier General) George S. Patton III, carried around a skull at his farewell party. A mother (opposite) weeps over the grave of her dead son.

"Search and Destroy"

American military efforts to "root out the VC infrastructure" by destroying their environment and removing their supporters were called "Search and Destroy" operations. (They still continue today, but are called "Search and Clear" to placate public opinion — the American public, that is.)

This is an account, written in 1967, of one such operation. It was fairly typical, neither the most bungled the author witnessed, nor the most vicious. Just one of the many thousands that served to confirm for the Vietnamese the identity of their enemies.

AERIAL VIEW of one of the villages of the Bantangan peninsula during the operation. Smoke rises from homes burning among neat, well-cared-for paddy fields.

In the whole of South Vietnam there is perhaps nowhere so lovely as the coastal region south of Da Nang. The provinces of Quang Nam, Quang Tin, and Quang Ngai delight the eye with their brochure beaches and lush paddy fields set against the backdrop of the mountains of the Central Highlands. Here, the paddy fields are smaller than those in the Delta and have many more villages scattered among them — tidy villages, cool under broad palm trees, pretty yet well planned. For space is at a premium, as over 90 percent of the population of these provinces lives along this fertile strip.

And in the whole of the region there is perhaps nowhere so lovely as the setting of Song Tra, at the mouth of the Song Tra Bong river. At least, the National Liberation Front must have thought so when choosing the site to build Song Tra as a model village. That was in 1962, when victory seemed certain. Their confidence even let them construct as many as thirty buildings of brick, a material avoided usually because of the danger of falling masonry during air and artillery strikes. They built a school, a health clinic, a community center, a pagoda, and even a Catholic church. There were four concrete wells (made, I was assured by a cynical American, with USAID cement) and an underground sewage system. For the fifty or so fishermen and their families living there, life must have been pleasant indeed.

Today, five thousand people rounded up by the American military from the villages of the adjoining Bantangan peninsula are held captive among the ruins of Song Tra. According to the official American view, these people have fled to freedom from the Vietcong who have been overtaxing them. In fact, though, the people from this area, like so many others in much of rural South Vietnam, have been solidly Vietcong—and earlier Viet Minh—since 1945. For the Americans, that was the problem.

From the "Bamboo Hut," which houses the officers' club on the seafront at the Chu Lai airbase, a major pointed at a cluster of lights out at sea. "See those fishing boats? Look carefully and beyond them you'll see the outline of a headland. It curves out until it just about overlooks our runway. And it's solid with Dinks."

(Dinks—the latest name for the Vietcong in this region.) "From there, they can hit us with mortars and rockets any time they like. So we're moving the people out and burning everything to deny food and shelter to the enemy. Then it'll be a free-fire zone." (In a free-fire zone, anything that moves can be shot.)

The area south of the airbase, down to the Song Tra Bong, has been considered "pacified" since the Marines landed there in 1965 and "cleaned out the place." This was when Song Tra, just over the river, was destroyed by Marine air strikes—"probably because it was a Vietcong showplace," speculated one soldier. The people who lived there that survived were brought over to the "pacified" north side of the river.

It was decided, in late August, to relocate the people from the peninsula into the ruined deserted village of Song Tra. Some preparatory work took place there: a platoon built bunkers on a hillside overlooking the village and two thousand people from the villages on the north side of the river were brought over to build a mile-and-a-quarter-long fortified fence around it. The bunkers—where, in the future, the Vietnamese Popular Forces which constitute "the Government Control" will be housed—together with the fence, will qualify Song Tra as a "New Life" hamlet.

The operation of relocating the villagers was planned in secret by Lt. Colonel Charles R. Smith, Jr., commander of the 4th Battalion, 31st Infantry of the 196th Light Infantry Brigade, part of Task Force Oregon. Before dawn, one company of Colonel Smith's men boarded Marine Amtracks (amphibious tanks) and Navy landing craft and headed toward the tip of the peninsula, while two other companies were lifted by helicopters to positions at the base to act as a blocking force against the escape of any surprised Vietcong. As the Amtracks approached the beach, loudspeakers blared out, "We are here to help you move to a new home. You will be given plenty of time and will be able to take with you as much

as you want. Our men will help you load your belongings and will assist you in any way possible. When you arrive at your new home, you will be given food, water, tools, medical care and protection!'' The hope of capturing any Vietcong in the trap quickly disappeared as the first light of dawn revealed scores of families, possessions packed, waiting on the beaches. Those Vietnamese who had been told of the operation were blamed for the security leak, and considering the large number of Vietcong sympathizers known to be among all Vietnamese troops, this was not unlikely. Most of the officers turned this disappointment to their advantage by insisting it showed how eager the people were to escape from the Vietcong, but the more cynical

GI's reckoned they were trying to be the first in Song Tra so as to get the best locations.

The companies met none of the opposition they had expected: no Vietcong were encountered at all, except for some long-range snipers later on in the operation. The relative acquiescence of the people was what was most surprising about the moving. They were being taken from land where, as animists, they had lived for generations, worshiping the spirits of ancestors buried there. And yet, as their houses were being burned and the Amtracks were tearing up the carefully cultivated paddy fields, there was no outward sign of protest — even at the most senseless destruction.

At first, only Amtracks and tanks with

THE ''ZIPPO'' SQUAD, named after the cigarette lighter used to ignite homes.

trailers were employed to move the people, but, as the lack of opposition became apparent, trucks were also used. As the operation continued, the following procedure became routine: Amtracks would plough a track across paddy fields to a village, followed by trucks; and then villagers, consisting mostly of women and children, would load up their household possessions — and, as the word got around about the shortage of building materials in Song Tra, as much as they could of that too — before the trucks moved on. The villagers did most of the work: in the beginning, GI's had lent a hand but soon found themselves carrying everything, with the villagers simply supervising. Occasionally one or two GI's helped in order to speed the villagers up, but, on the whole, they wandered about as little as possible for fear of booby traps. Most took things easy beneath the palm trees, issuing instructions to the villagers. Interpretation was done by the young Vietnamese boys every platoon seemed to have adopted. They came from over the river, near the airbase, and had picked up a working knowledge of GI-English. The nearest I saw to an angry Vietnamese was an elderly, white-bearded man being hurried up by a cheeky eight-year-old wearing a Marine helmet with a cigarette hanging out of the corner of his mouth. ''OK, number one babysan!'' encouraged a GI, ''you tell ole papasan if he don't get his ass outa here soon, he's gonna burn! I got my Zippo refueled real good last night!'' and he flicked his cigarette lighter on and off for all to see. Those members of the platoon whose job it was to set things alight seemed to genuinely enjoy their work and were always impatient to get it over with so as to be able to move along to the next house. This enthusiasm was not discouraged because the villagers tended to want to dismantle their houses completely and take them along, so the sooner the burning got under way, the sooner the platoon could move on. The result was that many villagers returned later, enduring the heat and smoke, to try to salvage possessions from their burning homes. Exactly why it was necessary to burn everything that remained, including the hay for the cows, was never explained further than: ''We got orders to leave nothing the Dinks can use.''

On arrival at Song Tra, everyone was at first screened by intelligence officers for ''Vietcong connections.'' Next, they were all registered, fingerprinted and photographed for their soon-to-be-issued identity cards (possession of which classifies the holder as a loyal supporter of the Government of South Vietnam and is, in effect, a prized safe-conduct pass). Each family was then directed to a site, nine feet by twelve feet, where it was told to build a house: for this purpose, tool-kits were issued to the heads of families. Children had bestowed upon them "Friendship Kits" which contain American candy and toys.

Once the people were allowed in, the race was on to erect shelters before the monsoon rains began. The plots were adjacent which meant that communal shelters had to be built, with a complete lack of privacy. Building materials were in short supply and so discarded army "C" ration cardboard boxes were used by some. One very sick old woman, considered "beyond hope" by the company medic, lay in the open under a piece of tarpaulin rigged up as a cover. Since there was not enough to make a door, she was destined to die there under the gaze of curious children. The whole scene was chaotic, with families and their livestock living together in the cramped spaces. Some, however, with characteristic ingenuity commandeered several bomb craters and used them as pig pens.

The health of the people was judged to be good by the battalion surgeon, Captain Mike Scotti, who had recently arrived in Vietnam from the Walter Reed Hospital. "They enjoyed a high standard of living in their villages and now, with this overcrowding, plague will be the problem." He explained there had been one hundred and sixty cases of plague reported the day before from a village nearby where people had been resettled. The danger is that when rats which have been playing host to the plague-carrying fleas die because of the burning of their food supplies in the villages, the fleas will pass on to humans. So, the whole of Song Tra has been sprayed with insecticide as a precaution. Also, everyone was tested for tuberculosis on arrival, but, unfortunately, with ineffective test material. As all Americans in Vietnam believe quite emphatically that the Vietnamese people never wash — in spite of the overwhelming evidence to the contrary — regular "wash-ins" were held to teach the people how to wash themselves, with predictable enthusiasm from the villagers.

When the last of the people had been moved, Colonel Smith and his senior officers took a final look around Song Tra before handing it over to the Vietnamese Popular Forces. The feeling was that it had been a very successful operation and Colonel Smith, a particularly sensitive

and conscientious man, appeared relieved it had gone so well. Unlike many military men in Vietnam, who hide nothing from the press because it never occurs to them that they have anything to hide, Colonel Smith seemed very much aware of what he had done and the censures of public opinion that might follow. Hence his insistence that the operation be carried out with as much attention as possible paid to the needs of the people. Given the task of defending the airbase, the choice became simple: since not enough men were available to occupy the whole of the peninsula to prevent the Vietcong using it as a base for attack, the alternative — to flatten everything and so deprive the Vietcong of cover — involved moving the people first. But, in South

A VICTIM of the "Food Denial" program.

Vietnam, people are not moved simply for their own safety, as Colonel Smith conceded when I asked why he thought the people seemed almost keen to leave. "They don't like our artillery and air strikes," he admitted.

And so it comes about that five thousand people, mostly women and children, are living in conditions variously described by two GI's in their bunker overlooking the village, as, "One big tinderbox, with all that thatch, one spark and the whole thing'll go up in a second!" "Hell no, man!" cried the other, "just wait until the monsoon really gets going—they'll be up to their eyeballs in mud."

It is intended (presuming the rains will keep the thatch damp long enough) that the people spend the rest of the war in Song Tra. In some ways, they are lucky, for it is unlikely that any more of them

will be killed by air and artillery strikes, and even if the USAID food supplies fail to get through or the alternative fifteen piasters (worth about two cents in purchasing power) a day they are awarded as "refugees" fails to get past the district chief, as frequently happens, they will not starve. The fishermen among them will provide something, and it is also planned to allow the people to return to their paddy fields to harvest their rice. With many of the dikes already destroyed by the Amtracks and the probable further destruction if bulldozers are used to flatten what's left, the chances of rescuing this season's crop seem remote. In any case, if defoliation spraying is used, it will certainly be lost.

What is likely to happen, judging by past experience, is that the population of Song Tra will slowly decrease. The disintegration of the old village society has already taken place with the disappearance of communal administration and religious ties. The fear and uncertainty which now holds the people together in Song Tra will lessen when, as time passes, the Popular Forces lose interest and enthusiasm and people will be able to slip away. Families will begin to split up and the village, as the fulcrum of Vietnamese society, will be destroyed forever. Wives and mothers will seek their husbands and their sons in nearby Vietcong areas. Some farmers will become fishermen, others will head for the American camps once they realize how easy it is to extract money from GI's. The prettier girls will have no difficulty getting work — whether it be "dusting" in the officers' quarters at the nearby Battalion or in the rapidly expanding brothels over the river. One girl had already set herself up in the engine room of the landing craft used to ferry GI's across the river: at a dollar for each five minute trip, she was earning more in a week than her father probably earned in all his life. The cause of the breakdown in society which permits such prostitution and delinquency to flourish, does not go unnoticed by the Vietnamese people and according to some it has become one of the most successful platforms in the Vietcong recruiting program.

Under these circumstances, it takes the blind faith of the convinced American to declare that people in Song Tra are now loyal supporters of the Government of South Vietnam. Nevertheless, officials in Saigon will inform the world that five thousand people fled the Vietcong to come to live in freedom in the "New Life" hamlet and that this is a clear indication that the war is being won.

BURNING HOMES—It is perhaps impossible for Americans, attuned to the idea of "mobile homes," to fully grasp the significance of moving Vietnamese from their ancestral lands. Nevertheless, one expected to find revulsion at the burning of homes instead of the party-like atmosphere that surrounded the operation. As the "Zippo" squad was moving on to the next group of houses, families attempted to rescue what they could from the flames.

CHILDREN watch as their world is being destroyed. Many of the homes in the Bantangan peninsula were well built and set in lush surroundings. Today most of the people are living under tin roofs and the peninsula is largely a free-fire zone.

EXHAUSTED GI (top), overcome by the heat (it was over 100° and hotter still for the "Zippo" squads), takes time off from burning homes for a smoke while a wounded girl (below), one of the few casualties during the operation, awaits medical help.

SMOULDERING REMAINS are all that is left as the last tank departs. Even hay for the animals was burned. Finally, artillery and air strikes were used to pulverize what remained. A mother consoles her child (opposite) as they leave their home forever.

Song Tra Epilogue

All that was in 1967. Three years later I went back to Chu Lai, by now famous as the home of the Americal Division (My Lai was a few miles south of Song Tra, on the Bantangan Peninsula). The "Bamboo Hut" was still there, now with an airconditioned bar. I waited there while the Press Information Officer arranged for me to revisit Song Tra. With my long hair, it didn't take much time for the two bar girls to start the questions: "You no GI! You civilian? How much you make? Bullsheet! You 'Maycan, you make beaucoup dollar!" (To every Vietnamese, a denial is absolute proof!) Then, in Vietnamese, I explained I was not American but British — it's the only phrase I'm fluent in and the only one I need to be fluent in. They froze with fear, trying to recall what they might have said for normally they could have been discussing plans to blow up the base with impunity, because hardly any Americans speak Vietnamese and any that do would reveal it immediately by trying it out to impress the bar girls. I put them at ease by saying I didn't agree with what the Americans were doing in Vietnam. Crisis over, the conversation continued: "You have wife? You like Vietnamese wife?" I explained that if it was dollars they wanted, why didn't they marry GI's? One leaned forward and whispered, "No can do! GI number 10. GI's kill beaucoup babysan, mamasan!"

That evening everyone watched "Midnight Cowboy," and in between shouts of "Right on!" from the younger men the sound of bombs falling on the headland across the bay could be heard, as the tin roofs of Song Tra momentarily reflected the orange glow of burning napalm dropping nearby.

Next morning, I was told that it was impossible to visit Song Tra. The Press Officer had been informed by the U.S. Commander for the area that it would take a company-size operation to enter because the village was "hostile." Eventually, a helicopter crew agreed to fly me over the place — they were warned, however, not to come below three thousand feet because of the danger of taking anti-aircraft fire.

The next day, at the U.S. Province Senior Advisor's office in Quang Ngai, during a briefing on the state of security within the province, I asked about Song Tra. Without hesitation I was told, "Oh, it's quite secure. It's a pacified refugee village."

SONG TRA in 1970, seen from 3,000 feet.

"VIETNAM ON THE MOVE," the "upbeat" phrase once popular with United States officials for describing the forced removal of the pe

"Relocation"

"Leaflets are dropped on four or five villages to say the village will be bombed in fifteen minutes — this is to give the villagers time to escape from the VC. We only actually bomb one of the villages, but we catch a lot of people running from the others!"

"But doesn't it mean that some villagers might not bother to leave one day if the leaflets haven't been correct before?"

"Any more questions, Gentlemen?"

Barry Zorthian, the U.S. Mission's chief press officer, during a press conference.

WHEN VILLAGERS are "relocated," the initial move is usually supervised by ARVN troops "because they can communicate with the people." In fact, their "high motivation" for the work is not unconnected with the looting possibilties afforded.

The war in Vietnam is a peoples' war and that is why the efforts of the American armed forces are irrelevant to the task of quelling it. The people struggle to defend their system of social values — their way of life — while America tries to impose a new one. To use GI's for this task is clearly nonsensical—"and counter-productive, too," as any USAID worker might add. No Vietnamese has ever had his mind changed by force.

Ultimately, the only way to win would be somehow to have an American living alongside every single family for the purpose of having him expose, by example, the hollowness of Vietnamese ideals of harmony and justice by acquainting its members with the delights of Americanism, typified, as one "unmotivated" Vietnamese cynically remarked — "by the electric toothbrush, the topless shoeshine girl, and the luminous (so you can find them in the dark) french letter. The outcome of such an experiment would not be questioned by most Americans, for how could anyone be blind enough to fail to grasp at a piece of the American Dream? The problem is only one of how to expose them to this new way of life. The American, with his life-style of technological trappings, could hardly be implanted within the village.

Instead, the solution has been to transplant the villagers into urban enclaves, which loosens them from their traditional values and makes the imposition of new ones easier. This policy, euphemistically called "relocation," is the one consistent aspect of American strategy in Vietnam. "Relocation" consists of destroying the fabric of rural society, using every military means possible to uproot the people and lay waste their homes for the purpose of creating a captive mass of people with their spirits broken in the hope of facilitating easier penetration with the new ideology.

This "restructuring" of Vietnam is carried on with indifference to human suffering and has by now incited sufficient hate among the Vietnamese for them to be convinced of the necessity of rejecting any values offered by those capable of such odious acts. Other than the sheer hypocrisy of pretending that the people are fleeing from the VC and "happen to be accompanied by GI's" — I once had a soldier, with the butt of his rifle in the back of a woman he was marching along, tell me quite seriously, "It's great to see these people voting with their feet" — the usual American explanation for the policy is that, from a military standpoint, the only effective way to weaken the guerilla is to remove his source of sustenance, that is, the peasants; to lay waste his habitat, that is, the countryside; and to call it "experiments with population and resources control methods." That this somewhat drastic measure is, in fact, militarily unsound has been proven by its ineffectiveness in hampering the guerilla. The food that has to be supplied by the U.S. to keep the peasants alive in their "refugee" camps and the money easily extracted from Americans who are always nearby to "protect" the camps is enough to enable sufficient to be passed on to the guerilla. Having civilians around their bases was thought by some U.S. officers to offer protection as they assumed the Vietcong wouldn't attack for fear of hitting the people. Instead, it was found that the people housed the guerillas, gave them intelligence information, and, on a night of attack, led them up to the perimeter of the base while girls distracted the guards.

The real goal of "relocation" is rarely mentioned: perhaps the clearest enunciation of it has come from Professor Samuel Huntington of Harvard, Chairman of the Council on Vietnamese Studies of the South-East Asia Development Advisory Group, who acknowledges that "in an absent-minded way the United States in Vietnam may well have stumbled on the answer to 'wars of national liberation,' " by "forced-draft urbanization and modernization, which rapidly brings the country in question out of the phase in which a rural revolutionary movement can hope to generate suffi-

AFTER LIVING for generations on their ancestral lands for which they have a special religious affinity, villagers are forced to leave, carrying with them what they can.

cient strength to come to power." In other words, when the Vietnamese are more worried about meeting the payments on their electric rice cookers than about what goes inside them the war will be won because the "American-sponsored urban revolution" will have succeeded.

VILLAGERS were rounded up, often taking with them only what they could carry. The more fortunate (top) managed to take a pig along. Many male villagers were usually held for days (above) for interrogation. The sign was incorrect for the only VC escaped during the night.

FORCED URBANIZATION was, and still is, the deliberate policy. Officially, the United States admits to "generating" three million "refugees," but this figure only covers the increase in population in Saigon and Danang alone during the period of American presence. The real number is at least twice that amount. Nowadays, as the war gets more automated, fewer "refugees" are encountered. The depopulation of the countryside is almost complete, and rather than risk GIs' lives bringing in any people that remain, it has become easier to bomb them.

INTERROGATION CENTER. During "relocation" operations, any males lucky enough not to be shot on sight end up in an interrogation center. This one in Binh Dinh Province had been hastily set up to "process" the vast numbers of men rounded up by the zealous 1st Cavalry Division. It consisted of an area marked off by barbed wire in which were packed over 200 "detainees." It had been raining heavily, but only about half of them, if they remained standing, could get under the only shelter, a piece of tarpaulin. Three days later they were still there, standing forlornly in a foot of water.

WORLD WAR II LANDING CRAFT, designed
amphibious assaults on Pacific beaches, came
of the mists one morning in January 1967 to t
away the people of Ben Suc who had b
rounded up on the river bank. While the villag
waited (previous page), eating breakfast in t
village for the last time, U.S. fighter bomb
searched for the sons and husbands hiding in
paddy fields. Everyone was moved, including
sick and the aged. The old woman above v
blind and had never before left Ben Suc. She s
her only concern was to return before she di
Opposite, a flotilla of landing craft on its way
the "refugee" camp.

CHINOOK HELICOPTERS were also used to move the people after they had finished their task of dropping CS "riot control" gas on areas of the "Triangle" where people might still be hiding. One helicopter (opposite page) had four such "gas drops" chalked up on its fuselage. Peasants (above) approach their new world through a dust storm caused by the helicopters. It was a piece of barren ground on which had been erected 40 long tents, in each of which 800 people were destined to live. The camp into which the people were concentrated was officially described as a "center." It was surrounded by barbed wire and at the entrance was a sign saying "Welcome to Freedom."

ARRIVING VILLAGERS pass bars and brothels on the road outside the camp (top left). In the camp, the "Psy-Ops" officer discovered h
had forgotten to order "indigenous reading material," and, to prevent "boredom," he distributed old copies of *Playboy* magazine to the people

THE "REFUGEE" PROBLEM was greatest in the northern part of South Vietnam where the concentration of U.S. troops was highest. By 1966, more people were already living outside the official camps than inside them. In Quang Ngai, about 200 took over a partly constructed cathedral where, because of its central location, many prostitutes worked. Men at the nearby MACV compound recommended visits to the "only place in the world where you can get a 'short time' behind the high altar." The breakdown of family life and the people's misery are regarded by the various evangelical relief organizations as heaven-sent opportunities to make new converts. Religious conversions coincided with news of the arrival of a shipment of rice for a Catholic camp. Another group trained barbers, as if short hair were the road to salvation. Yet another organization saw the sewing machine as an updated version of the Gandhian spinning wheel — every cardboard shack seemed to vibrate with one.

Despite the official line that the people were there because they "heroically refused to live with the communist knife at their throats," those like the officer below recognized the resentment — not once did he take his hand away from his pistol while in the camp. In and around a bombed-out church near Duc Pho (opposite) lived 300 people, "resettled" there at the end of 1970. ("Resettled" is the latest word being used in the hope of deceiving the U.S. public into thinking the "relocated" people are being allowed back to their homes.)

A few days earlier, some men from the local MACV compound stopped their jeep in front of the church. A 14-year-old boy threw a grenade into the jeep. "It didn't explode," explained one man, "We had to M16 the boy through, blew him to pieces."

GOVERNMENT POSTER attached to the barbed wire fence of a "refugee" camp that serves as a constant reminder of the hazards of

age would be foolhardy enough to fly the Vietcong flag, and no pilot was ever deterred from dropping his bombs by not seeing one.

"Our Vietnamese Friends"

MAJOR GENERAL Ngo Quang Truong, Commanding General 1st ARVN Infantry Division; Colonel David Lownds, Commander 26th Marine Regiment; and Major General John J. Tolson III, Commander 1st Cavalry Division, at Khe Sanh meeting.

Amidst all the rhetoric about "saving Vietnam from the Communists" one fact is always conveniently forgotten, and that is that Vietnam once had a Communist government. Furthermore, the people chose it — on January 6, 1946, during the first election ever allowed to the Vietnamese. While it can be observed, correctly, that they thought themselves to be voting for leaders more nationalist than Communist, no one has ever tried to deny that the voters were fully aware Ho Chi Minh was also a Communist.

It is obvious that this one fact completely negates America's stated purpose for being in Vietnam, because America can hardly claim to be helping the Vietnamese choose the kind of government they want when they made their choice years ago. When this information is presented to Americans in Vietnam, the reaction it provokes is very interesting. It is almost as if, years ago, someone in Washington realized what difficulties such information might cause future Americans and so manipulated events to provide some contradictory evidence.

This evidence seems very plausible and admirably serves its purpose of justifying American involvement in Vietnam by purporting to establish the presence of a sizable number of anti-Communist supporters of the government ruling in Saigon. The degree to which this unique viewpoint is accepted is directly proportional to one's ignorance of Vietnamese history, which is to say that all but a handful of Americans seem to accept it. So, when they are confronted with this evidence of the elected Communist government of 1946 as proof of the hollowness of the GVN's claims to wide popular support, their reaction is sheer disbelief, and in rebuttal they offer the familiar fact of the exodus from Communist North Vietnam to South Vietnam after the Geneva Accords in 1954. Now this sounds convincing until one discovers that most of those who left were followers of a foreign faith, Catholicism; and they had a bad record of collaboration with the French, which alienated them from the nationalists who had just gained power. With the promise of an

easier life in the south under the newly installed Catholic Prime Minister Diem, it can be assumed that all Catholics in the north would have wanted to go south; but, despite the pressure to do so from the Church and American Psychological Warfare experts, whose contribution was to drop leaflets saying the Virgin Mary had gone south and all the faithful should follow, only about two thirds of them, seven hundred and fifty thousand, actually did. (Like all statistics in Vietnam, this one too has been exaggerated — President Nixon still talks about the one and one-half million Catholics who fled south.) The U.S. Government, having put Diem in power, was naturally anxious to provide him with some supporters; so, units of the Seventh Fleet were engaged to ship them south and almost one hundred million dollars was provided to cover moving expenses.

Thus, these Catholics from the north, these alienated people, cut off from the mainstream of Vietnamese society yet wielding power far out of proportion to their numbers thanks to their preferential treatment under Diem, are deemed, by those ignorant of history, to be the most important pro-American faction in Vietnam, for whom abandonment to the Communist would be "a bloodstain on the conscience of America." They have been the foremost recipients of American aid, literally showered with handouts — one U.S. colonel regularly flew over Catholic villages in his helicopter throwing out Hershey bars ". . . just to remind 'em how we appreciate their loyalty." In return they tell the Americans what they want to hear — by now the action is purely reflex in the Pavlovian fashion: a tirade of anti-Communist rhetoric while the right arm jerks into outstretched position, palm uppermost. What becomes apparent after seeing this degrading spectacle repeated over and over again is the obvious insincerity of what's being said and the very real contempt and hatred for the Americans. Alienated from other Vietnamese by religion and courted so passionately by Americans, they are in the position of the whore who hates her clients while not being able to resist their money. For despite the evidence of religious tolerance towards Catholics in North Vietnam those in South Vietnam have convinced themselves (perhaps by telling Americans so often) that a bloodbath will follow a Communist takeover. Therefore they tend to engage themselves in short-term industries like black-marketeering and prostitution which produce ready cash for sending to banks abroad, rather than in long-term projects under the U.S. "nation building" program.

DAUGHTER of a GVN official, resettled in the south from Hanoi, in 1954.

Apart from the Catholics, the only other groups that even pretend to support the American aims in Vietnam are the minority religious groups. (The other exception is the Montagnards, hill folk of Malayo-Polynesian stock, who are prepared to support anyone who'll give them weapons to defend themselves against the Vietnamese by whom they are hated.) The minority religious groups are the Hoa Hao and the Cao Dai, both of which have been subjected to the full force of the USAID "planned seduction" policy, not to mention outright bribery for their anti-Communist stand. Most Americans, as they proudly stride around such areas as An Giang Province, the bountiful home of the Hoa Hao, now bursting at the seams with American aid, would be surprised to learn that the pro-American smiles they received were in no small part due to orders from their leaders who have been paid in greenbacks for their loyalty. Instead, their ignorance of the history of the Hoa Hao enables them to see An Giang Province as *the* great success story of Vietnam. In fact, it is, but for the Communists! This is because An Giang Province provides food for all the VC regular main force units in the Delta. The province is strategically situated between the two VC staging areas, the Plain of Reeds and the U Minh forest. In return for accommodating the Americans — which involves smiling at them, offering cups of tea at every opportunity, smiling even when they refuse, and interjecting remarks like "VC, number 10!" (VC, very bad) at least once a minute — they have had their material lives enriched beyond belief by USAID handouts. And in return for supplying them with food the VC leave the Hoa Hao alone — which is to say that there is no visible sign of a VC infrastructure so the province is spared the death and destruction the U.S. military dispenses elsewhere. The cost of the food is more than adequately compensated for by the increased production afforded by free seed, fertilizer, and machinery which is donated by the U.S. There is no shortage of manpower because the population has not been decimated by firepower and the sons of the Hoa Hao are not often drafted into the ARVN. GVN officials sent to round up draft-dodgers are unable to gain entry into the Hoa Hao areas because of the powerful autonomy created by the direct provision of American wealth. The result is that both the Hoa Hao and the Vietcong are happy, and, thanks to their naïve ignorance, so are the Americans.

For into this lush barbed-wire-less par-

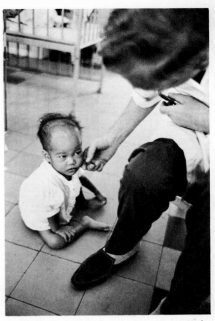

GI'S abandoned son in a hospital.

adise are brought plane-loads of shaken pacification workers with looks beyond anything tranquilizers can do to help. From all over Vietnam they come, from the furthermost unfriendly fields where the farmers shoot first and smile later, to nearby "contested" areas where no one, not even those lucky recipients who qualify for the most generous gifts under the "accelerated animal protein production program," ever smile. Snatched from suicidal states, they are whisked off in the nick of time to be shown the promised land. In a trance they are led by the hand through throngs of ever-smiling people to stroke and pat fat pink-eyed American pure-bred pigs who smile back contentedly from familiar brick-built sties. On over picturesque concrete bridges they go (here the USAID cement is not used for building VC bunkers), into lush Elysian fields swaying with IR8 miracle rice, ripe and eager, being cut by more smiling people striding behind their individual two-stroke diesel rice-harvesters. On down canals in motorized sampans between fields throbbing with new high-yielding agricultural technology, passing yet more smiling, waving people, this time covered in suds from the handout "Dial 24-Hour Protection" soap as they take their evening bathe. No need to leave before nightfall: the war is no more real here than a nightmare and the only shooting will be during "Gunsmoke," on the TV set provided under the "New Life Development Program," in the village chief's house.

In retrospect, perhaps, An Giang Province is needed by Americans — it certainly makes them very happy.

"MOTIVATING" the American soldier to fight was cause of great concern. One view was that they should be made to stay until the war was won. Considering what carnage was caused by somewhat lazy and good-humored GI's, the Vietnamese people can only be thankful for their lack of "motivation." For almost all GI's it was simply a question of trying to stay alive for 365 days to catch the "Freedom Bird" back to "The World" (the plane back to the United States). Strategically, the presence of GI's has achieved nothing, apart from assuring that Vietnam will be communist. Unfortunately, the extent to which Vietnamese society has been destroyed means that the future communist regime can afford to be very authoritarian indeed, for the people will now accept anything that gives them order and justice. The most visible result of the GIs' visit is the spectacle of the maimed and wounded, a sight difficult to avoid even when off to catch the plane home. Enticements and rewards were offered, many in the Madison Avenue tradition (opposite).

CRISTMAS IN VIETNAM. Orphans (opposite and top) visit a United States Army hospital to sing and dance for the wounded men whose predecessors were responsible for these childrens' parentless status. The Nativity scene (above) is from th Saigon USO club.

BEACHHEAD ASSAULTS took place more often for drunken parties than for attacking the enemy. As the war became more automated, soldiers who remained had more leisure time. By late 1970 the beaches were ablaze with the fires of barbecue grills.

SAIGON WATERFRONT. In keeping with its position as the fountainhead of consumerism in Vietnam, its homes are dominated by adverti

APPROACHING SAIGON by road (above), the peasant is confronted with advertisements and watchtowers, the pillars of urban life, and also with policemen, whom he has to bribe to be allowed entry. Three and a half million people live within the city, built to hold 350 thousand. Unlike other countries, where industrialization has caused predictable population shifts to the cities, Vietnam has no urban industries to offer. There is a shortage of food, which is conveniently met at the moment by importing surplus U.S. foodstuffs.

The only industry that exists in Vietnam is the "servicing" of Americans. This is a very degrading occupation for any Vietnamese (it is pleasing to note they make very bad slaves), but in the new society dictated by the United States, everything possible is being done to hasten the transition from proud farmer to humble cyclo-driver. By a process which relies on the insecurity felt by the peasant in his alien surroundings and his fears for the future in a money-based society where the money daily depreciates in value, the peasant is being reminded constantly that wealth, not wisdom, is the supreme virtue. The overall result is a mass of resentful people, unified in the common task of extracting the maximum amount of money from the Americans in ways which, if questioned, they would deny being capable of.

They beg (right), live in inhuman conditions (opposite), and all the while feel trapped and cheated, for they can still remember what human dignity is all about. With what clarity they do remember is revealed by the sight of a father, convulsed with tears, retching in the gutter, clasping the money he's just earned for spending half an hour in an American's hotel room.

THE MAIN SQUARE in the center of Cantho (opposite) where families live in shacks made from old C-ration boxes. The main street in Nhatrang (top) and the ultimate sacrilege, a graveyard in Danang which is now being used as a communal lavatory.

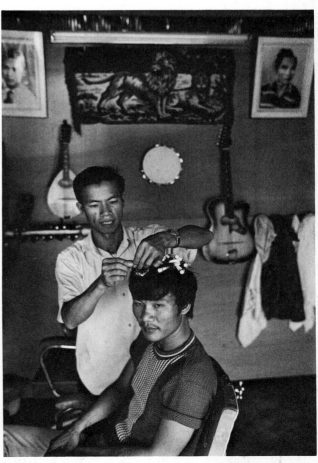

SAIGON STREET SCENES. "Bunny girl" (opposite) on movie poster. The traditional *ao dai* is giving way to the miniskirt (top left). Bust of student heroine (top right). Some people beg while others get their hair done to become entertainers of Americans.

CROOKED MONEY-CHANGERS (top) often pass off toilet paper wrapped in 500-piaster notes. Wealthy family (above) lunch at their pago

ORSHIPPERS at Le Van Duyet's tomb (top), which is the grave of the military hero where thousands come to pay homage to their ancestors.

ICI REPOSE
Notre petite fille ch
Michèle BOSSÉ-BER
le II Juin

CONCESSION
DE 15 ANS
LE II JUIN 1952

GRAVEYARDS were taken over by the newly arrived residents in the congested towns and cities. (Saigon is said to have the highest population density of any city in the world.) Despite living conditions in the urban centers, the inhabitants could constantly console themselves that at least they were safe from the death being rained down on those who remained in the countryside. Somehow, amid the over-crowding, the rats, and the disease, they survived, even with a certain poise — like the girls in their spotless white *ao dai's* who glided like swans between mounds of rotting garbage, seemingly oblivious to the stench surrounding them.

PPREHENSIVENESS is the national characteristic. The Vietnamese possess a taut, nervous energy. On the streets they miss nothing. 116

PEANUT GIRLS. A face-saving form of begging — the GI pays but is persuaded by the girl's hurt expression to refuse the peanuts.

Air Force Major Chester L. Brown circled above the town for hours directing the air and artillery fire onto the homes below. Eighty-five percent of the town was destroyed (overleaf) during the three-day battle to drive out the VC.

School children of Ben Tre in happier times (top opposite) and what remained of the marketplace (opposite) after the attack by American firepower.

"It became necessary to destroy the town in order to save it."

THE BATTLE FOR HUE. During the Tet offensive, the fiercest fighting took place in the old imperial capital of Hue. The reason was twofold: Hue was the only town or city in Vietnam with existing fortifications — the 20-foot-high, 6-foot-wide walls of the citadel — which offered protection against air strikes; also, during much of the 24-day battle, bad weather prevented close air strikes. These two facts served the Vietcong: first, by enabling them to reap the propaganda value that came from holding a U.S. "sanctuary" for over three weeks; and second, by giving them the opportunity to show how Americans were prepared to destroy a national monument, revered by all Vietnamese, by the use of indiscriminate artillery and naval gunfire. When the weather improved, the standard "close air support" tactic was employed. This involved dropping 750-pound bombs and napalm on the center of the city. To the inhabitants of Hue, the U.S. troops seemed to act like madmen who had an uncontrollable passion for killing communists, without a second thought for the civilians they killed.

Marines (opposite) run for cover while under fire from a VC pillbox which had somehow survived despite dozens of direct hits from bazooka shells. Movie poster (above) in the main street damaged during the fighting.

THE MARINES were sent to retake Hue. Having barely got used to fighting in the paddy fields, they now found themselves engaged in the highly specialized business of street fighting. Although it was a task that called for stealth and mobility, they trundled around as conspicuously as the men on the moon. For the shortest of trips they traveled on "mules" — the "mule" is a sort of military golf cart — which made them very vulnerable to snipers. Inside the citadel U.S. air and artillery strikes failed to "suppress" the VC entrenched in the solid walls, so progress was slow, even non-existent on some days. From the walls, most of the streets could be seen, making it easy for the VC to fire rockets at the tanks upon which the Marines relied so much.

Unfortunately, many Marines were killed by accident. With justified contempt for the standard U.S. rifle, the unreliable M16, some Marines took to using captured AK47 weapons. When fired, these make a distinctive sound. This labeled the owner VC by those who could not see him. Hence, Marines threw grenades and directed mortar fire at the sound, killing their comrades. In all, about 200 Americans died in the process of replacing the VC flag — which had flown for three weeks over the citadel — with the Stars and Stripes.

In addition, 7,500 Vietnamese are thought to have lost their lives. The official U.S. line is that 3,500 of these, the civilians, were assassinated by the VC before the remaining 4,000, the VC themselves, were killed by Americans.

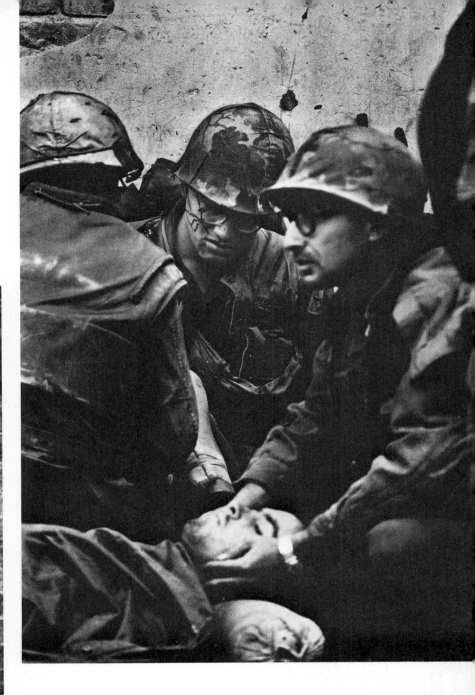

THE STUNNED PEOPLE of Hue became refugees within their own city. Traditionally proud and independent, they watched with horror as U.S. and ARVN troops tore the city apart. Seventy percent of the homes were destroyed and almost every one was looted.

REFUGEES flee across the broken bridge at Hue. Marines intended it to carry their counterattack from the southern side right into the c

e the many guards, the Vietcong were able to swim underwater and blow up the bridge, using skin-diving equipment from the Marines' PX.

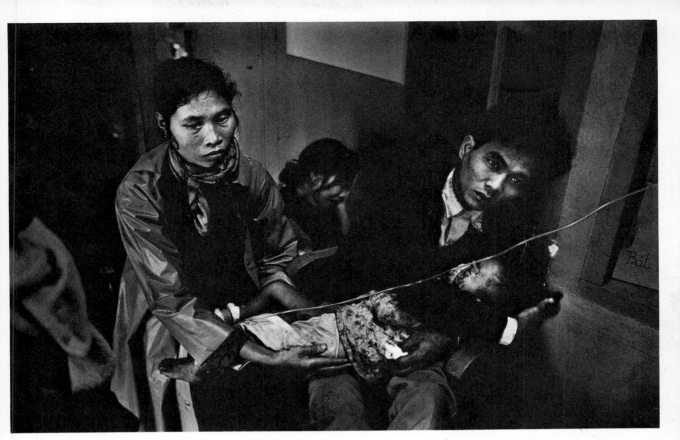

CIVILIAN CASUALTIES. Many took refuge in the university. An old man (opposite) died in one of the lecture rooms, his family around him. Many waited, wounds unattended (above), while the more fortunate (top) got as far as the operating-room door.

OTHER CIVILIAN CASUALTIES were the result of the indiscriminate use of firepower — naval gunfire from the 7th Fleet which had been called in to knock out snipers. The 750-pound bomb crater above was in one of the main streets. People buried their dead wherever they could. The grounds of Hue University (top) became a graveyard. Students help to dig a grave to bury a woman's husband whose corpse lies in a coffin made out of USAID "gift package" container still bearing the clasped United States—Vietnamese handshake greeting. Inside the battered citadel (opposite), a woman burns incense at a grave.

The Battle for the Cities

UNTRAINED for and unfamiliar with street fighting, many Americans were killed.

To the people of South Vietnam and America, Tet 1968 marked the point when the American involvement in Vietnam lost its credibility. To the American people, who had continually believed the ultra-optimistic progress reports on the war, it was this news from Saigon that destroyed their faith in the honesty of their leaders. To the Vietnamese people, caught up in the battles, it was the final disillusionment.

What the Tet and May offensives did was to negate the central premise on which the logic of the relocation policy is based. This is that the urban centers are havens from the death and destruction meted out those still living in the countryside. In the spring of 1968 this fallacy was exposed. The sacrifices villagers had made in leaving their ancestral lands for the horrors of city life were in vain. With grim irony, the very same pilots who had bombed them out of the countryside were now bombing them in the cities. The sanctuaries were no more.

That the success of guerilla warfare depends largely on outwitting the enemy is no secret except, so it seemed, to the American military machine. Not only do the Vietcong rely upon this ignorance to score the more conventional military "wins," but also to manipulate the Americans into unwittingly helping them to achieve their objectives. At no time was this more plainly seen than during the Tet and May offensives. In fact, it was particularly obvious even to those correspondents in Saigon who'd allegedly "got it all wrong about the war due to sitting drinking on the roof-bar of the Caravelle Hotel instead of getting out in the paddy fields." For the roof-bar of the Caravelle offered a grandstand view of the Phantom jets dropping bombs and napalm on the homes of the only pro-American Vietnamese in Saigon.

That the Vietcong should have launched their attacks on the towns and cities of South Vietnam during the spring of 1968 was a logical and predictable step and the degree to which one was surprised by it was directly proportional to the extent one had believed the U.S. Information network: officially stated, the war was being won . . . the VC were on the run . . . the NVA were dying like flies trying unsuccessfully to assail Con Tien . . . the previous autumn's battles for Hill 875, Dak To and Loc Ninh were a crushing defeat for the enemy . . . and so on. The gullible have never been the same since they woke that fateful morning in January to find the American Embassy swarming with Vietcong.

To the more cynical, the facts presented themselves more clearly. There is evidence that in the late summer of 1967 it was apparent to the VC that the Johnson administration would settle for peace talks and that eventually some kind of cease fire would result. This would be tantamount to a victory for the VC, provided the population realized they would be negotiating as *de facto* victors. The population in the countryside needed no convincing for they were already aware of which side was winning. The urban population, however, had been subjected to a three-year barrage of propaganda through radio, television and newspapers, which said the VC were on the run and the GVN in control. These people had to be made crystal clear about who was really succeeding, and the method chosen was the coordinated attack on the towns and cities, for so long heralded as sanctuaries invulnerable to VC attack. To bring this about it was first necessary to hoodwink Westmoreland into thinking that Phase Three of Giap's offensive had begun, so conventional battles between main-force units were initiated near the borders with the purpose of drawing away U.S. troops from the urban areas. NVA units, supposedly ringed around Khe Sanh, were actually miles away consolidating themselves for the Tet attack on Hue!

The Tet offensive revealed the power of the VC and the extent of its popular support, while discrediting the claim of America to guarantee protection to its supporters. The U.S. command comforted itself with what has by now become the standard method, that of attributing nonexistent goals to the enemy and then taking credit for denying it these goals: in this case, it was claimed that the VC had failed in trying to start a general uprising which would take over all South Vietnam and push half a million American troops into the sea. The VC, to make sure that no one would believe Tet had been their "final fling," (as Westmoreland had claimed and backed up with an incredible "enemy killed" figure) launched the second offensive in May. In Saigon, it was aimed particularly at convincing the Catholic community and, to a lesser extent, any Chinese in Cholon who might still think that the Americans could offer protection.

All it took to destroy District 8 was a handful of Vietcong . . . and help from the U.S. Army and Air Force.

CRUCIFIX rescued from bombed home.

13

District 8, on the southern edge of Saigon, had been reclaimed from swampland and built up with the aid of American money under a "community action" program. It was a showplace, with a steady stream of visiting senators being shown what *could* be done. What had been done was everything that the Americans were capable of: it was the ultimate manifestation of their best efforts in Vietnam. What existed in District 8 was the nearest thing, in Vietnam, to a well-to-do middle class in the American image. The people were Northern Catholics who had come to live in the South after the Geneva Accords. Under Catholic President Diem they fared well and with their "northern industriousness" virtually took over the civil service. Thus, District 8 had become the success-story district, full of anti-Communist, pro-Government Catholics. Homes were substantially built, with little of the overcrowding that can be seen in the rest of Saigon. Houses had electricity and water supplies, and, to the delight of the ARVN and U.S. troops who later "liberated" the area, were full of expensive consumer goods. GI's, who'd previously been lucky to find more than a red pepper in deserted homes out in the paddy fields, found themselves with more TV sets, radios, tape recorders and refrigerators than they could carry. (Some did manage to empty a warehouse full of airconditioners — a theft which was quite seriously attributed to VC guerillas).

For the VC to alienate the people of District 8 from the Americans proved simple since it turned out that the U.S. Air Force might just as well have been under the operational control of the Vietcong. The method chosen was for a small group of VC commandos to enter the area and adopt the "Xuyen oc" tactic, which means "fighting through the houses" (first used by the Viet Minh against the French in the December 1946 battle of Hanoi — an event with which the U.S. military command was apparently unfamiliar. Holes are cut through the adjoining wall of houses — compensation being paid to the owner on the spot — so that the guerilla has maximum mobility and many vantage points to fire at the attackers). The battle started with the VC shooting a policeman, which, any Vietnamese will agree, is a good way of starting anything. The police then called in the ARVN, whose main concern was to evacuate the people so they could start looting. The gunfire to be heard was mostly the ARVN shooting locks off doors, but it was interpreted by the U.S. advisor to the ARVN company as "heavy contact" and the ARVN were told to pull back so that U.S. helicopter gunships

REFUGEES fleeing from their burning homes pass a poster showing how the "Free World Forces" quash the VC.

could "work over" the VC positions. Those inhabitants who were skeptical of the purported VC strength and reluctant to leave behind unguarded valuable possessions were the ones to be killed. When, in frustration, the U.S. replaced helicopters with artillery and with air strikes by jets dropping seven-hundred-and-fifty-pound bombs and napalm, the VC had achieved their goal. Shots heard fifty yards away would cause the artillery to be called in although it could have been a clip of bullets exploding in a fire. The VC had banked on an over-reaction, blitzkrieg fashion, by the soldiers, untrained and unfamiliar with house-to-house fighting. In addition, the employment of U.S. ground troops in District 8 was particularly unfortunate, in that it enabled the people to identify Americans with the destruction.

After the spring of 1968, a mood of apathetic resignation settled in among the Vietnamese. Their total disillusionment with American promises left a resentment that has never been erased. The Americans have never understood this, preferring to believe instead remarks like the one spoken by a U.S. 9th Division Captain upon surveying the destruction his men had wrought: "The people know it was Charlie's fault. They know we had to do it to save them from the VC." The Vietnamese, presumably not bright enough to follow this brand of veracity, came to the conclusion it was American helicopters and bombers that destroyed their homes because the VC don't have any. And so, by their cleverness, a few dedicated men revealed the hollowness of America's claim to the allegiance of the people of South Vietnam; and at the same time, ensured by their manipulation of the American military machine, that any pockets of allegiance were neutralized.

The extent of the efforts to counter this setback made by the American Mission in Saigon consisted, first, of denouncing the VC as sneaky for attacking during a truce, despite the fact that the truce had been canceled by the Saigon administration; then, second, of claiming to have decimated the VC forces, who, unfortunately, reappeared, their morale as high as ever, to launch the May offensive; and, finally, of running an unprecedented propaganda campaign to present the casualties of the fighting in Hue, most of whom were killed by the most hysterical use of American firepower ever seen, as the victims of a Communist massacre.

DURING TET, GI's for the first time witnessed the urban elite being killed.

THE BATTLES FOR SAIGON. At Tet and again in May, the Vietcong struck Saigon. They aimed for the middle-class districts which were duly destroyed by United States firepower. Looting was extensive, so people fled with everything they could carry.

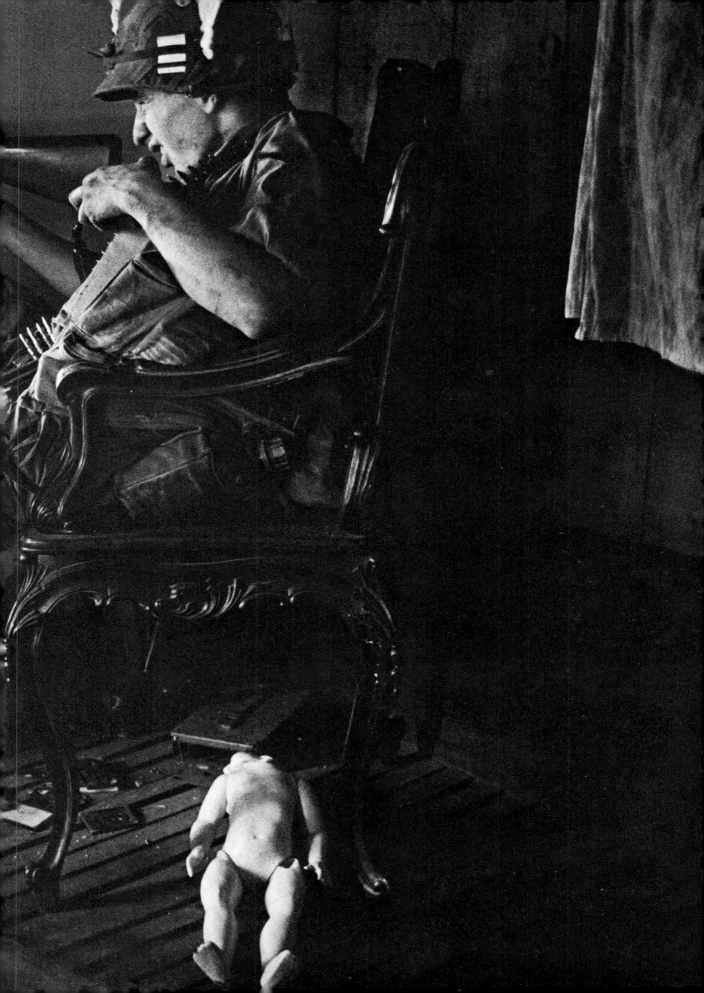

U.S. TROOPS were used to retake Saigon, but only after ARVN soldiers had first tried and failed. The woman opposite was killed by U.S. helicopter fire the day before as she ran out of her home to grab her child. The U.S. troops were from the 9th Division and had spent the whole of their tour wading through the mud of the delta. Some GI's were amazed to see multi-story buildings, and many were sobered by the realization that they were now destroying the homes of people who, in some cases, enjoyed a higher standard of material comfort than they themselves did in America. The looting was staggering. The ARVN, who had entered the areas first, had taken everything that could be carried by hand. The GI's, with their APC's, were able to take away refrigerators, TV sets, and other heavy items. Each evening they could be seen unloading their vehicles for sleeping. This procedure had been made a rule after two GI's were killed by an enemy mortar round on the first night because their APC was so full they had had to sleep outside.

THE PROBLEM with "close" air and artillery support is that it can often be too close. The troops above and right had cordoned off a block. After much firing from behind their tanks and APC's, they decided to call in artillery fire from their base camp. The first shell sent everyone diving into their vehicles; the second left two GI's dead and three wounded. If there was a Vietcong sniper around he missed a lot of easy targets, for after the artillery stopped, the GI's stood in exposed groups, utterly dejected, telling each other what awful torture they had planned for the artillery officers back at their camp.

WOUNDED CHILDREN, who, like most civilian victims, had been hit by indiscriminately used U.S. firepower. The boy below was on his way to church in a ''safe'' area when helicopters, firing onto some VC positions only 300 yards away, overshot a rocket and wounded him. He died later in the hospital. Unlike the peasants in the countryside, the people of Saigon were less inhibited in making their anger felt. ''Why Americans crazy? Only four VC! Americans bring many helicopters — destroy everything!'' screamed one man, shaking with rage after having witnessed U.S. airpower reducing a whole block to flaming rubble. A 9th Division captain explained that all areas that might be occupied by VC would be destroyed, for this was the most economical way of saving American lives.

FATHER carries his wounded son (opposite) past those American troops who fired the shots. (They had mistaken a horse for a Vietcong, and had sprayed the area with gunfire.) GI's (top) recover after narrowly escaping death at the hands of their colleagues who gave them somewhat inaccurate covering fire as they retreated along a ditch from a Vietcong sniper.

FIRES WERE STARTED deliberately to drive out the VC, occasionally with napalm, but usually one helicopter tracer bullet was eno

nited States has given the Saigon government a fleet of fire engines, but they are too wide to enter the narrow streets where most people live.

AFTER THE FIGHTING WAS OVER, the people were allowed to return to their former homes — or rather what was left of them. The government paid each owner twenty dollars compensation, that is if the owner was still alive. The high number of civilian casualties was in part due to the fact that Vietnamese homes offer little protection from the large-caliber bullets which are fired by helicopters. Most houses have thin tin roofs and the walls are made of the fragile hollow bricks favored by the Vietnamese because they keep the houses cool. Unlike the peasants in the countryside, the people of Saigon felt no need to build bunkers under their homes for they never anticipated being bombed and strafed.

technological self-deception ever.

HES relies upon having information about every hamlet, and the task of providing this is undertaken by the American Senior District Advisor. It is no exaggeration to suggest that it would be unlikely for him even to get the hamlet's name correct—President Diem had a renaming spree in the 50's which has meant that many hamlets have a real name and a given name, much to the delight of the Vietnamese who consider ambiguity a virtue. Ultimately, it is the character of the peasants which negates the whole system. For they esteem secrecy as much as Americans esteem frankness.

When the District Senior Advisor arrives in the hamlet, the interpreter he brings along will almost certainly be a North Vietnamese. He will speak a dialect which, first of all, the people will have difficulty in understanding and, second, will identify him as a Northerner whom they, as Southerners, will distrust. If the Advisor happens to be one of the very few who can speak some of the language himself, the same will apply since almost all the language instructors for U.S. personel are North Vietnamese. Armed with a list of one hundred and thirty-nine questions, the District Advisor and his interpreter will thus try to get the answers the computer needs.

The first problem encountered will be a vagueness by the Vietnamese when it comes to expressing quantity. For the peasants have a nonmathematical view of the universe imparted, it is thought, by the Buddhist concept of immediacy —"what exists now is the only reality." Thus, many a farmer, when asked how

"PHOENIX" PROGRAM, the other side of "pacification"—interrogating a farmer.

many children he has, will answer "two," pointing at a couple in front of him and ignoring his other eight working in the fields. Asked his age, the reply is often "very old," or just "old," and when pressed it might be "forty and some years." Alternatively, some will simply offer their ID cards for examination with an "if they're so interested, let them read what they typed on the card" attitude. Asked if the date of birth on the cards is correct, they won't know. In reply to further questioning, they will own "a little land"; work it with "some buffalos"; and spend on fertilizer "one thousand and some hundreds of piasters." Were the farmer to know the exact answers, it is doubtful if he would reveal them. (A forthright answer would be rejected automatically by another Vietnamese as a proof of lying!) Being taunted and ridiculed for not knowing exactly what he owned would make him warm inside with an introspective glow of newly found importance. This secretiveness is instinctive and is treasured, for it has enabled the Vietnamese nation to remain intact for two thousand years.

Against this background can be judged the wisdom of trying to get answers to questions like, "Does your household have a member or members who participated, by coercion or otherwise, in enemy-organized nonmilitary group activities (public meetings, demonstrations, work gangs, etc.) during the past quarter?"

These computer questions not only have an almost surrealistic quality, but also they offer an insight into American

notions of what should motivate the Vietnamese. For a glimpse of the American vision of a "restructured" Vietnam, these examples are offered:

"Do any households in this hamlet own a TV set?"

"Are there any organized activities for the youth of this village (4T, boy scouts, sports, etc.)?"

"Do any households in this hamlet own *motorized* vehicles (such as motorcycles, motorized sampans, cars, etc.)?"

"Can Western medicines, particularly the more common antibiotics, be purchased locally by village residents?"

"Is there a surplus of goods or foodstuffs produced in the village for sale outside of the village?"

It is the answers to these and similar questions that have enabled the U.S. Mission to assert that the government in Saigon controls the vast majority of the people of South Vietnam. Deduction of this "fact" from the answers to such questions is due, in no small way it seems, to the application of the Bayesian scoring algorithm, which is, I was assured, "used to successively integrate the weights associated with responses to each of the component questions in order to establish the final grade to be assigned a particular hamlet for a given model." This may well be the case, but, as "HES 70 is a highly integrated man-machine interface," it would be fortunate if someone on the "man" side realized that the system measures "control," not "allegiance," which is not the same thing at all!

FARMER'S DAUGHTER awaiting the verdict of the Phoenix's kangaroo court.

GIFT from GI's. Peasants are puzzled that grown men carry so much candy.

PERSONAL HYGIENE — particularly that of the Vietnamese — was always a matter of great concern to Americans. Every American seemed quite convinced the people were somehow "unhygienic." On the other hand, the Vietnamese, who found it necessary to bathe three times a day, could never understand why Americans restricted themselves to only daily washing. The Marine (above) was demonstrating to bored mothers how to bathe a child. One mother realized the Marine was using her vegetable dish to stand the boy in and, to the embarrassment of the other Marines, grabbed the dish and strode off, cursing such disregard for the basics of cleanliness. U.S. officer (top opposite) gives candy to village children. Marines (opposite) conduct impromptu dentistry.

THE COMPUTER that ''proves'' the war is being won. Data collected for the ''Hamlet Evaluation System'' is analysed by it to ''see who loves

...istic results on the "my-wife-is-not-trying-to-poison-me-therefore-she-loves-me" pattern are reliably produced each and every month.

"REVOLUTIONARY DEVELOPMENT CADRE," the CIA-supported contribution to "Pacification." Young people are trained in the best Maoist tradition by ex-communists to win the allegiance of peasants. The program is run by a Colonel Be, who was thrown out of the Vietminh, he says, "because they found me too revolutionary." His cadres go off to proselytize villagers, using the same techniques as the VC; they dress like the VC and sing almost identical songs about "power to the people." (Were it not for the fact that they steal chickens, some people probably would be confused as to which side they were from.) Many Americans regard the program's major achievement to be that of confusing the peasants. Unfortunately for the cadres, the peasants are not alone; many newly arrived GI's have opened fire on the gun-toting, black-pajamad cadres. At an award ceremony (above), cadres salute against a backdrop of exploding smoke bombs. President Thieu (opposite), himself once a communist district chief, questions a cadre.

VICE-PRESIDENT KY (above). Electioneering posters (top) being erected. Elections were run by Ky's old school chum, Nguyen Duc Thang

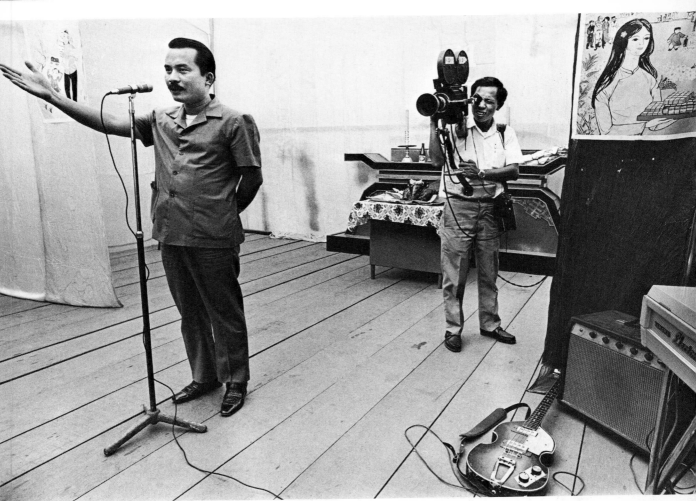

GENERAL WESTMORELAND (top). Chieu Hoi minister (above), a northerner who became tearful when defectors sang old VC marching songs.

DEMONSTRATIONS are very popular in Saigon. They all have one thing in common — they are ignored by almost all Vietnamese who realize, quite correctly, that in the police state of South Vietnam no genuine demonstration can ever take place. The ones who do participate are generally either Catholics, paramilitary youth groups (Ky's "Anti-Fraud Group" was the most violent of these, consisting of some 400 pardoned criminals, each given a taxi by Ky in exchange for allegiance), war veterans, or "students." Apart from domestic political reasons (as when Thieu allowed the war veterans to go on the rampage, barri-cading themselves in and shooting American MP's, so that he could then prove his indispensability to Ambassador Bunker by quashing them), the main purpose of demonstrations is to show the outside world how fascist the Saigon regime is. It is as if the GVN are so anxious to see Americans leave Vietnam, they are implementing a deliberate policy of disillusionment. Their chief spokesman is still Nguyen Cao ("Hitler was my hero") Ky, who diligently continues his task of making Americans question the nature of the society the United States is trying to save in South Vietnam. Ky is from North Vietnam.

Soldiers (above) display banners carefully written in English for the foreign newsreel cameras — signifying to the perceptive viewer that if soldiers need to demonstrate for war, the people must want peace. A girl (left), demonstrating against those fa-voring peace, marches in a torchlight procession. The torches were U.S. soft-drink cans stuffed with flaming rags. The military statue in the center of Saigon (opposite) was built by students of the *Social Realist Grotesque* school, a style rarely encount-ered outside the Soviet Union. It was erected in a few days using "Kwik-set Cement." One soldier sprayed it with black paint while the other applied green to the corners to give the statue a weathered bronze look.

LIFE IN THE CITIES after the Tet and May offensives of 1968 took on a different quality. Until then, a certain resigned kind of order existed based on the acceptance, however reluctant, of the logic of living in the cities rather than dying in the countryside. After Tet, however, the people felt cheated and trapped. The Vietnamese, with their highly organized existence, have always had a safety valve to use in the face of disaster, which allows persons to dispense with responsibility for their actions — "everyone's meter is switched off." Further, if no leader exists who possesses the "Mandate of Heaven," the "natural order" (which comes to be as a result of harmony between "man and state") simply ceases. Thus, after Tet, the people felt free to act just as they felt, while they waited for the leader to appear. As of July 1971, they are still waiting, and still shocking foreigners with their outrageous behavior. (This, of course, applies only to those few Vietnamese who do not accept that Ho Chi Minh was their naturally chosen leader.)

On the streets of Saigon, guns are everywhere. Under the guise of looking for VC guerrillas, soldiers and policemen complement their meager salaries by extracting money by threat from the public. Motorcyclists are regularly victimized — any who try to get away are shot at. (This impresses Americans, who see it as a much-needed traffic control measure.) An exhibition of captured weapons after Tet (top opposite) served to confirm the strength of the VC. People mused that if the inefficient ARVN could have captured this much, then the amount they didn't find must have been staggering.

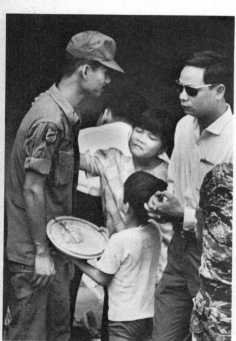

PICKPOCKETING was how some Vietnamese snatched at the "green dream." What was surprising was not so much the existence of pickpockets (although the Vietnamese are traditionally very honest) as the toleration of them by the public. Hatred of the Americans was such that no Vietnamese would ever warn one if his wallet was about to be taken. In fact, many people could be seen surreptitiously admiring pickpockets' prowess, and Vietnamese policemen always released them if they were caught. More commonly (above left), the oldest girl member of this particular gang would allow herself to be caught to enable the others to get away. She was able to escape every time since no American would struggle with her for long when she started to shout, "No can do, GI, me too young, you too big!"

PREVAILING ECONOMIC CONDITIONS make it necessary for all Vietnamese to steal, simply to live. The closer they are to Americans with their "waste economy," the easier it becomes. For workers in the huge American bases, opportunities are unlimited, but detection and the resulting humiliation can be severe. Workers are herded like cattle (below) through check-out gates where they are searched and anything found on them is confiscated — even something they may have picked out of a garbage can. After extolling personal property as the goal of life itself, Americans cause puzzlement by seeming so anxious to frustrate Vietnamese efforts toward that end.

GARBAGE DUMPS. Traditional Vietnamese society produces no garbage or waste of any kind; even human excrement goes straight into the family fish pond to feed the fish. Today, conditions in Vietnam would bring a gleam into any "Earth Day" marcher's eye. The Americans produce a colossal amount of garbage, and a lot of what they throw away the Vietnamese value and are prepared to buy. The peasant children (above) were playing in the fields when a U.S. truck came along and dumped its load. A new garbage dump was born and the curious children examined its strange contents. By now, like the mother and daughter opposite, they are probably making a living salvaging some of the debris. This work is dangerous, as GI's sometimes booby-trap the garbage, feeling the Vietnamese should not be taking it.

In Danang (top opposite), outside the U.S. airbase, is the longest dump in Vietnam, perhaps in the world. It burns continually. A truck carrying a load of coffins drives past through the smoke. In Cantho (opposite), in the main square, a pig roots through garbage piled high in the center of the town.

17

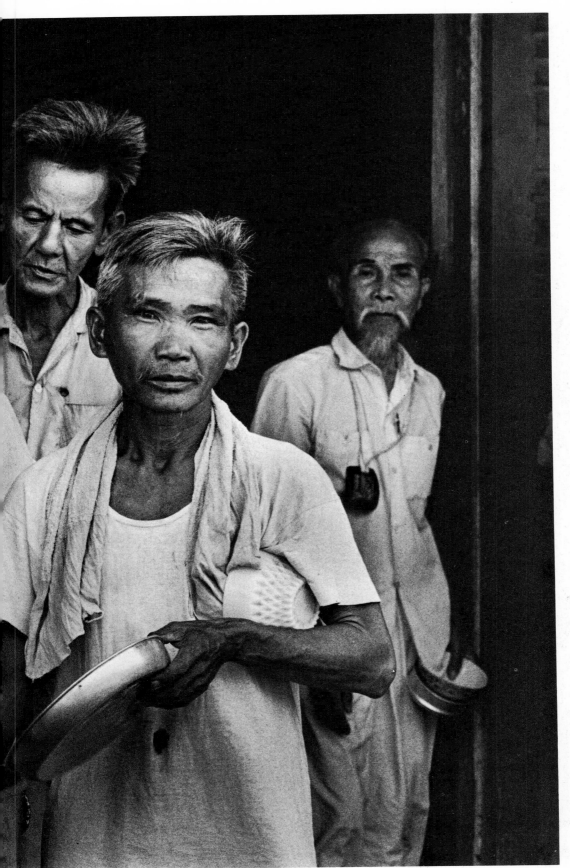

THE ELDERLY are traditionally cared for by younger members of the family. Nowadays, with the upheavals caused by the war, many old people live out their lives in institutions. This one, on the outskirts of Saigon, is run by a group of Catholic sisters. In return for much praying, the old men are fed rice from a communal bin placed outside their dormitory.

THE WOMEN OF VIETNAM. In a society where they are traditionally revered for their poise and purity, women have been effectively dehumanized. They sit outside American bases waiting to enter to serve the soldiers as everything from laundrymaid to prostitute.

A BEAUTIFUL DAUGHTER can be a bonanza for a poor family. She can sell "girlie paintings" until she grows old enough to join her sisters.

VIETNAMESE GIRLS, despite their great beauty, make very bad whores, as they know nothing of seduction and hate their clients. Possibl
the most unliberated women outside Islam, they are thrust into prostitution from as early an age as twelve (top) and always hate it

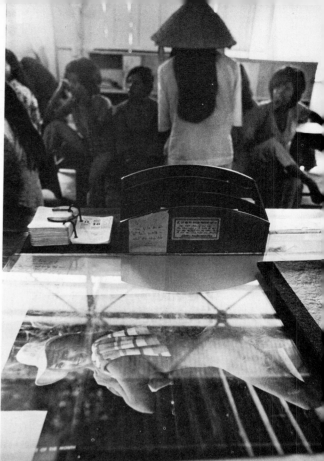

PENICILLIN AND PLAYMATES (top) in a VD clinic run by the American Navy. Two thirds of the local bar girls were generally found to be infected with the disease. Despite such realities, the sailors and GI's are helped to feel as much at home as possible (above

THE PRESENCE of GI's has served to emasculate Vietnamese men. They have been relegated to the roles of pimp and procurer, and as a result they have the greatest contempt for the wives, sisters, and daughters whom they sell so readily to GI's.

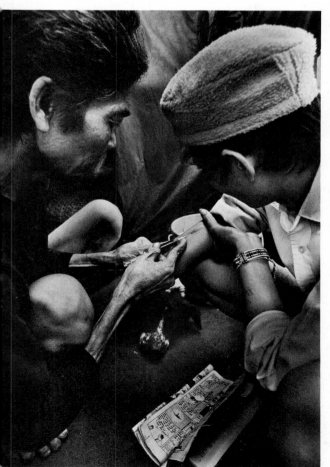

COUNTRY BOY (above) becomes a pimp for girls in a brothel set in a paddy field to accommodate a U.S. Engineering Battalion newly arrived in the area. Schoolgirls in Saigon (opposite page) on their way home pass drug addicts who get their injections in full view of the public. Although opium smoking is a long-established practice in Vietnam, injecting heroin is a more recent innovation, introduced by Americans. The number of addicts is increasing rapidly, even among young boys, as each day there seems less reason for living.

For those men who do not turn to drugs for relief, resentment turns to an anger that is directed at any American they see. With the full approval of every other Vietnamese, they cheat Americans, steal from them, and quite frequently kill them. With U.S. troop withdrawals under way, their desperation increases as the basis of wealth in the urban enclaves, the American dollar, ceases to flow. Their other great fear is of not being able to reestablish their former autocratic status with the women. As over half a million girls have "cohabited" with Americans who, for the most part, treat them with far greater respect and understanding, the Vietnamese men anticipate difficulties.

In order to counteract the first criticism a girl might make on returning to a Vietnamese, the men have spread a rumor that Americans have brought to Vietnam the "shrinking bird disease" ("bird" is a euphemism for penis), which only afflicts Vietnamese men because the Americans are innoculated against it.

DISCARDED EQUIPMENT collects in huge stockpiles as the ground war draws to a close. Helmets (top) discarded as too big for Vietnames

GE PROFITS are made by merchants who resell scrap, even wooden boxes for artillery shells that Vietnamese buy for building houses.

THE AUTOMATED WAR

BACK IN THE UNITED STATES, dead GI's gave the war a bad name, so that by 1968 Nixon's electioneering pledge had to include a promise "to bring the boys home." The efficacy of air power in depopulating the countryside was indeed so great that this promise was easy to keep. But not until the Cambodian invasion of 1970 did the military leaders finally grasp the futility of employing American ground troops. GI's were never needed — a company of Girl Scouts would have sufficed, provided they could use a radio and a map to inform the pilots when fired at by the enemy. By today, even this function is obsolete, for there now exist electronic sensing devices whose information is passed through computers that automatically launch artillery or air-strikes.

The shape of things to come was predicted by General Westmoreland in 1969: ". . . enemy forces will be located, tracked and targeted almost instantaneously through the use of data links, computer-assisted intelligence evaluation, and automatic fire control. With first round kill probabilities approaching certainty, and with surveillance devices that can continually track the enemy, the need for large forces to fix the opposition physically will be less important."

Aircraft carriers are an integral part of the new warfare — they are the United States' invulnerable sanctuaries on the sea. They have never been attacked by the enemy but still have many casualties through accidents. This man (opposite) walks through flames in his asbestos suit to rescue pilots.

"YANKEE STATION" is the area in the South China Sea where the United States carriers position themselves for bombing runs on Vietnam

THE SAILORS and the pilots on board have never been to Vietnam. They have never seen the faces of their victims, the Vietnamese people.

BOMB-LADEN PLANES are catapulted off the deck. Intended for emergency use in far-off conflicts, carriers are wasteful of men and machines.

e accident rate is high. This one carried two different size planes: the smaller often fell in the sea on takeoff and the larger crashed on landi**r**

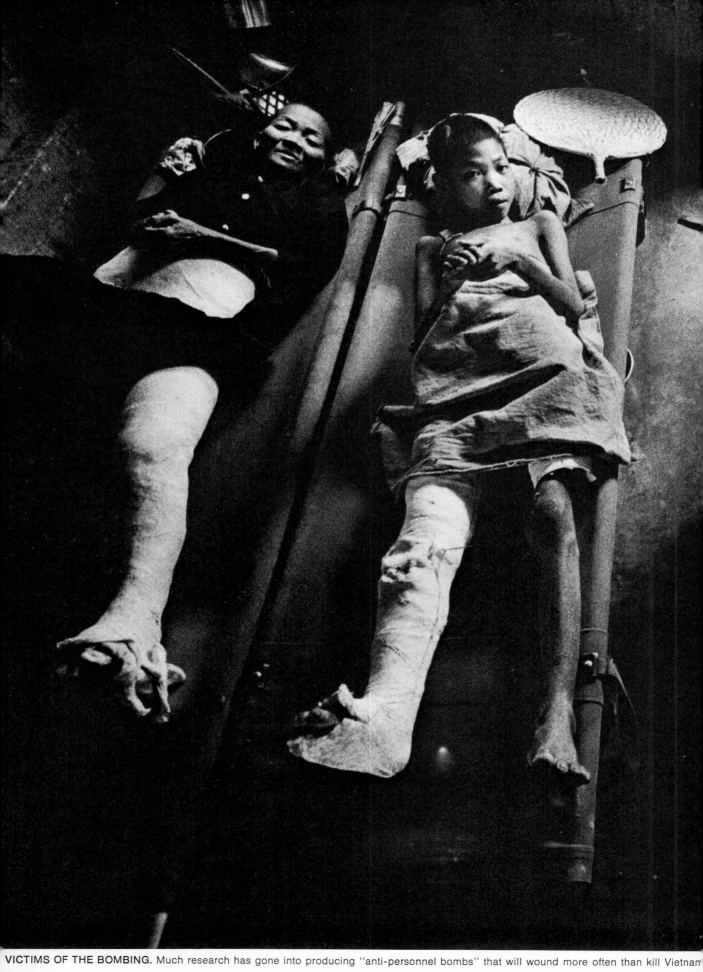

VICTIMS OF THE BOMBING. Much research has gone into producing "anti-personnel bombs" that will wound more often than kill Vietnam

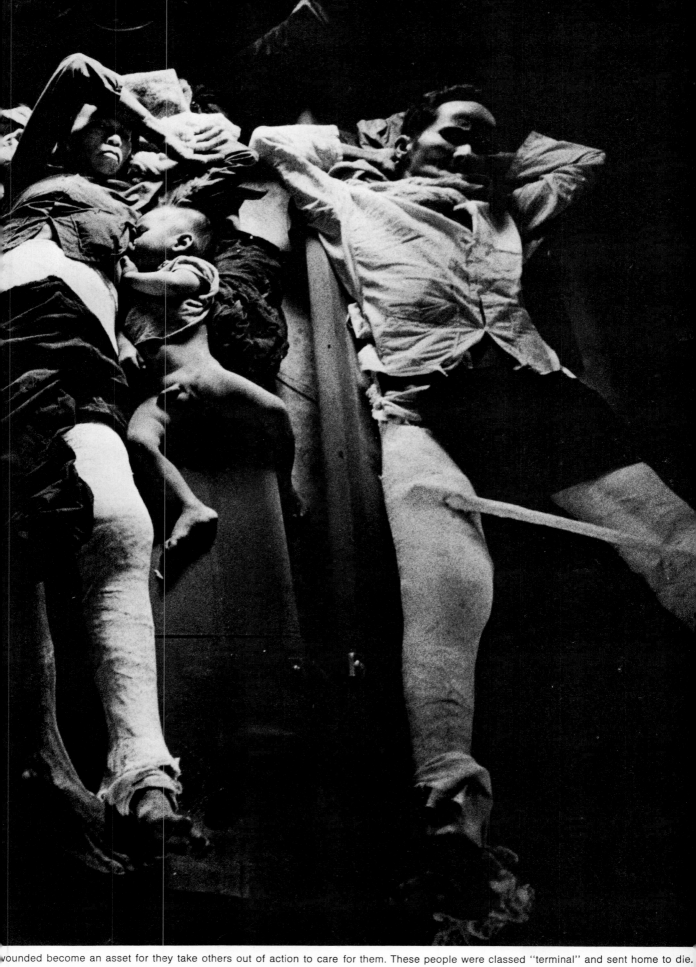

wounded become an asset for they take others out of action to care for them. These people were classed "terminal" and sent home to die.

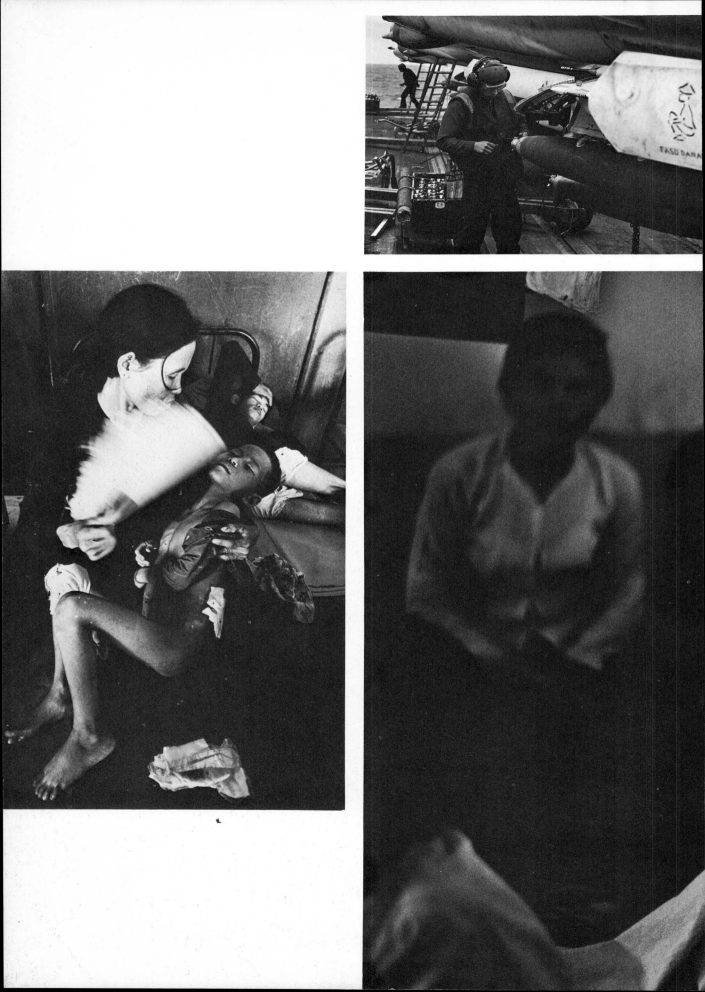

MAIMED CIVILIANS, the result of the indiscriminate use of American firepower, will be a notable feature of the Vietnamese population for years to come. The lack of doctors and specialized surgical techniques has caused the adoption of amputation as a time-saving measure. On the GVN side, there is no "public medicine" — doctors treat only the wealthy. The peasants are cared for by foreigners working for the various relief agencies. However, as most of these work with Vietnamese interpreters, peasants still have to be able to raise money to bribe the interpreters before they can get past them for treatment.

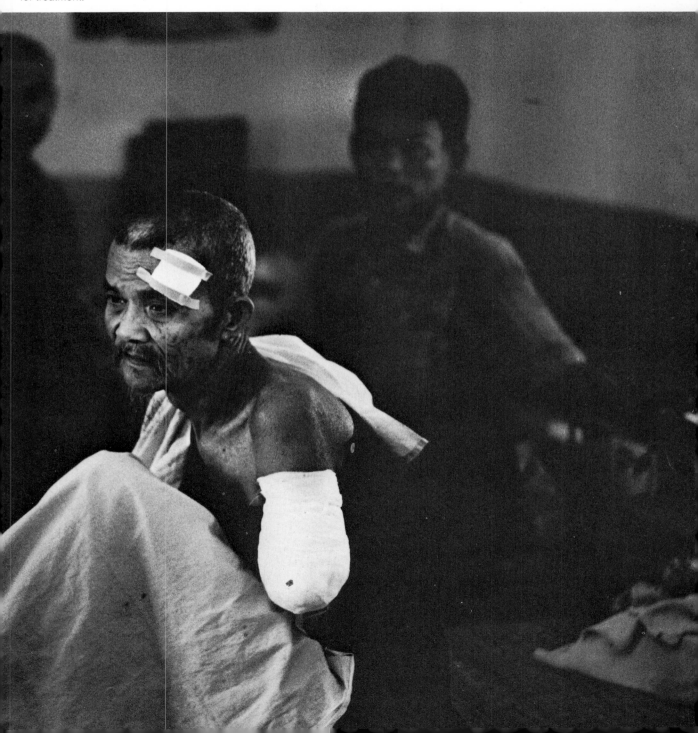

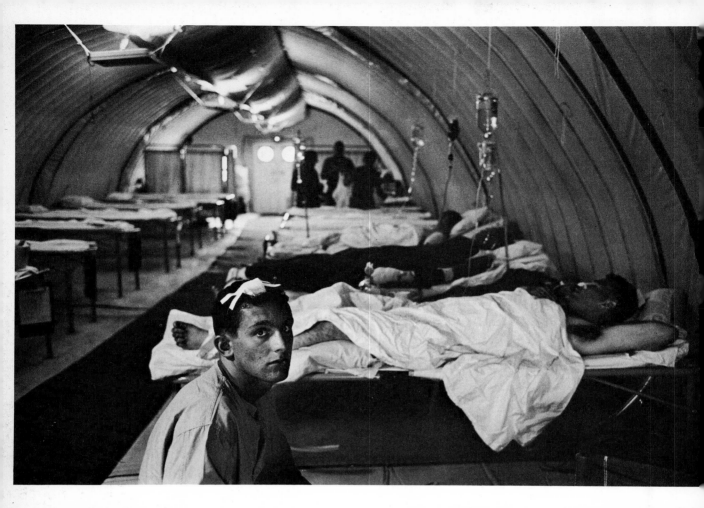

THE WOUNDED. Perhaps nothing more clearly reveals the extent of American indifference toward the suffering of the Vietnamese people than the enormous disparity between the money and effort expended to kill the Vietcong and that used to treat and care for civilians wounded — in theory accidentally — by U.S. forces while being protected from the VC. Wounded GI's (above) had the best medical care possible lavished upon them, but the Vietnamese (opposite) were allowed to lie dying in desperately overcrowded hospitals. Patients died simply for want of intravenous fluids or just someone to administer them.

At Quang Ngai Province Hospital in 1967, the only available surgeon, a European, turned up each morning after curfew and had to decide which of the newly arrived casualties (victims of the night's artillery fire) had a chance. Every morning he played God, deciding who would live and who would die. He hated the role but he knew that he could not possibly operate on them all and that it was better to spend time on those who might pull through.

He and his assistants worked like demons in the operating room during the daylight hours (there was no electricity — and no running water), cursing as air strikes 1,000 yards away shook plaster from the ceiling onto the open bodies on the operating table. Working under such high pressure, they accidentally set the boy's broken arm (right) the wrong way. A month later he was still waiting to have it reset.

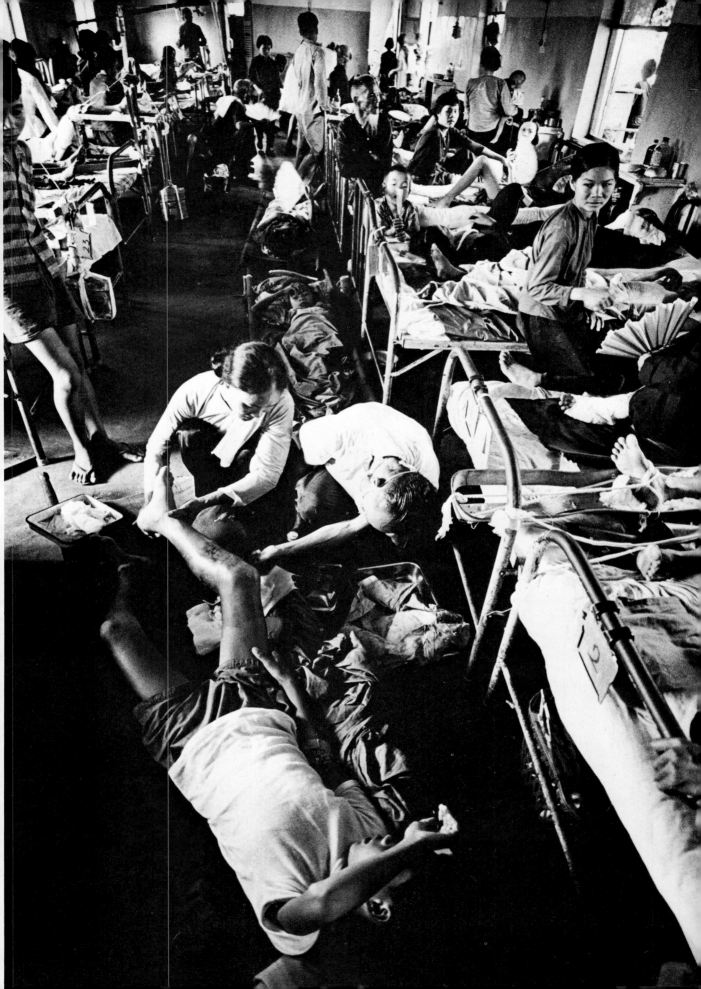

AMPUTEES are fortunate if they can get fitted with artificial limbs. There are only three centers in all of South Vietnam, and only one of these, the one run by the Quakers, is situated where it is most needed — in this case, in battle-scarred Quang Ngai province.

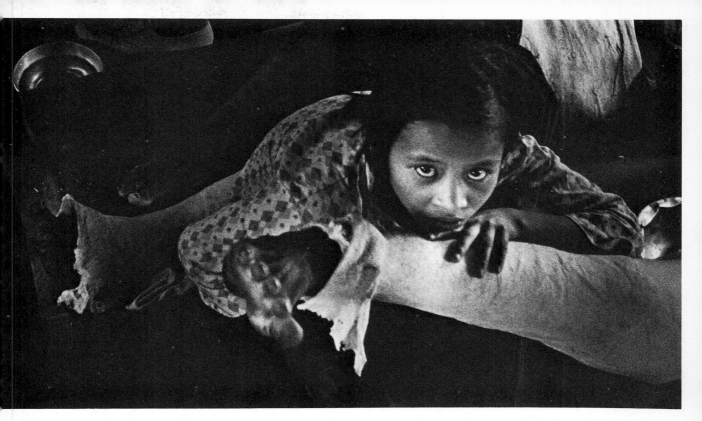

IS HALF-VIETNAMESE, half-Indian boy (above), living in Saigon, was wrongly accused by the police of being a thief. To prove his inocence, retain his self-esteem, and maintain his dignity, he chopped off his little finger in front of them. He now wears it around his neck.

NAPALM. The most effective "anti-personnel" weapon, it is euphemistically described as "unfamiliar cooking fluid" by those apologists for American military methods who automatically attribute all napalm cases to domestic accidents caused by the people using gasoline instead of kerosene in their cooking stoves. Kerosene is far too expensive for the peasants, who actually use charcoal for cooking. The only "cooking fluid" they know is very "unfamiliar" — and is delivered through their roofs by U.S. planes.

Some of its finer selling points were explained to me by a pilot in 1966: "We sure are pleased with those backroom boys at Dow. The original product wasn't so hot — if the gooks were quick they could scrape it off. So the boys started adding polystyrene — now it sticks like shit to a blanket. But then if the gooks jumped under water it stopped burning, so they started adding Willie Peter [WP — white phosphorous] so's to make it burn better. It'll even burn under water now. And just one drop is enough, it'll keep on burning right down to the bone so they die anyway from phosphorous poisoning."

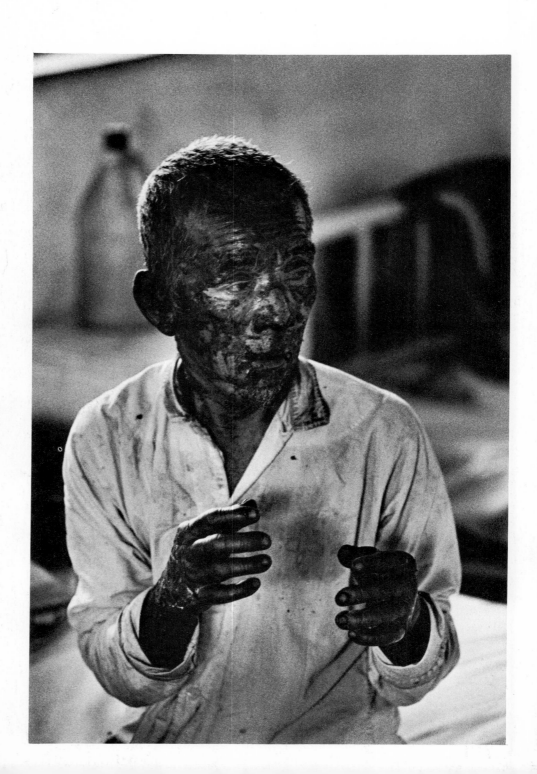

PAGES 211-212 ARE MISSING

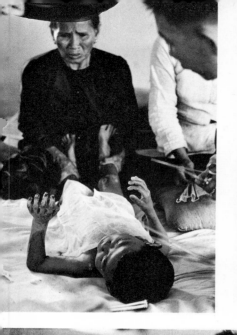
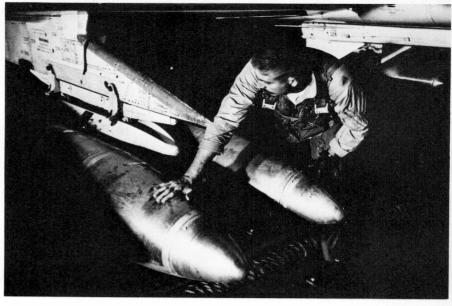
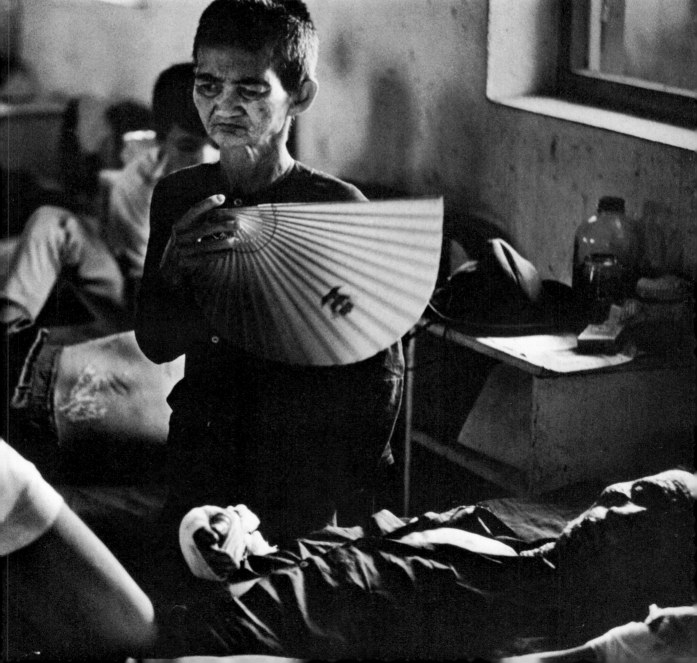

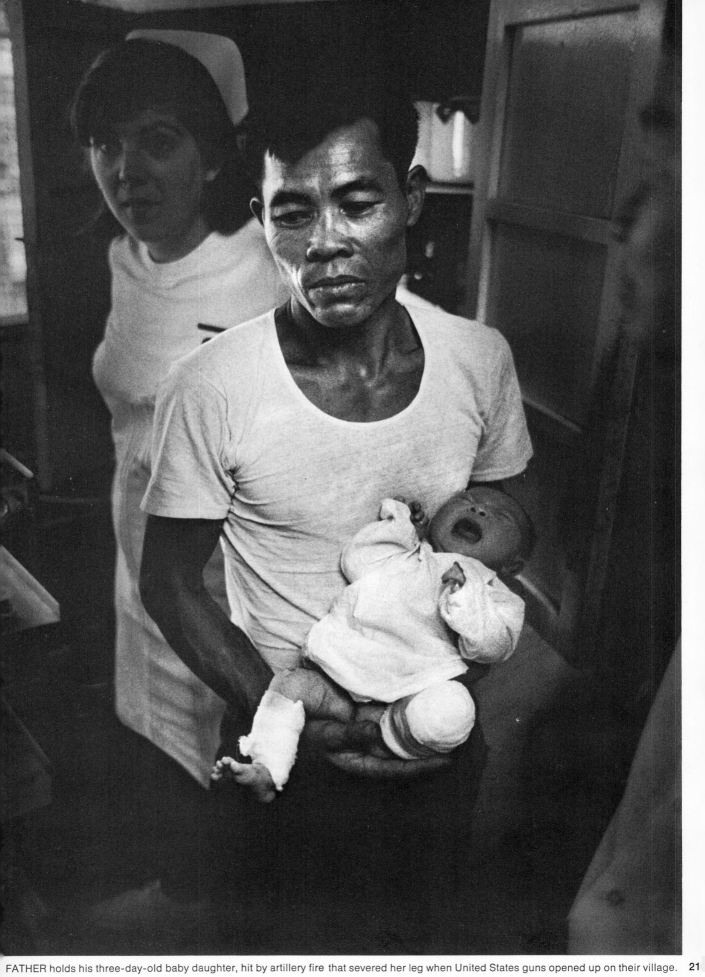

FATHER holds his three-day-old baby daughter, hit by artillery fire that severed her leg when United States guns opened up on their village. 21

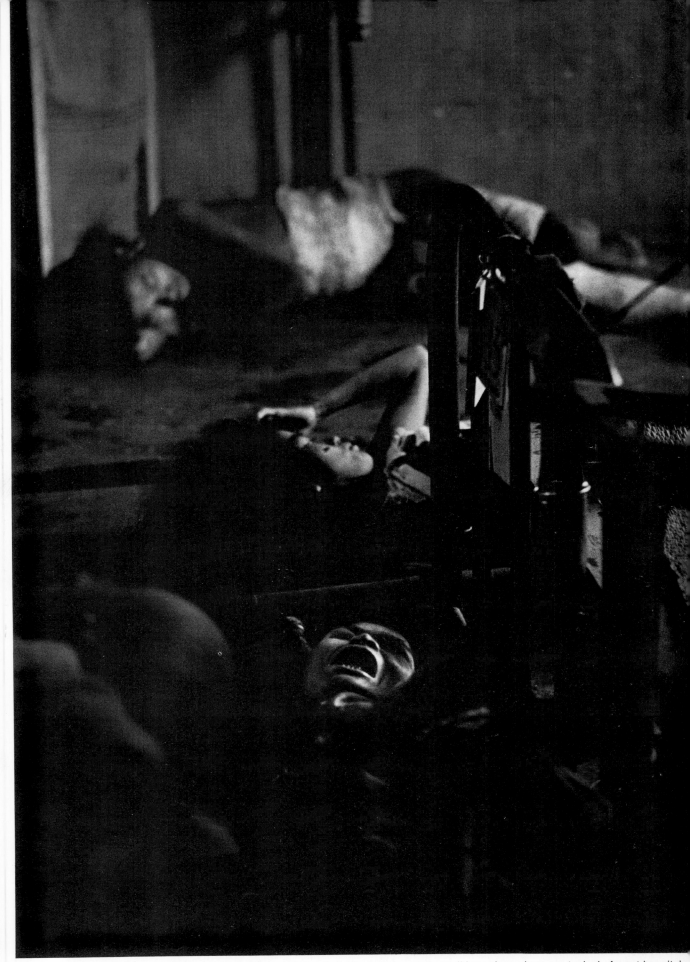

215   PATIENT screams on a hospital floor as her leg wound is treated. The overcrowded conditions shown here are typical of most hospitals

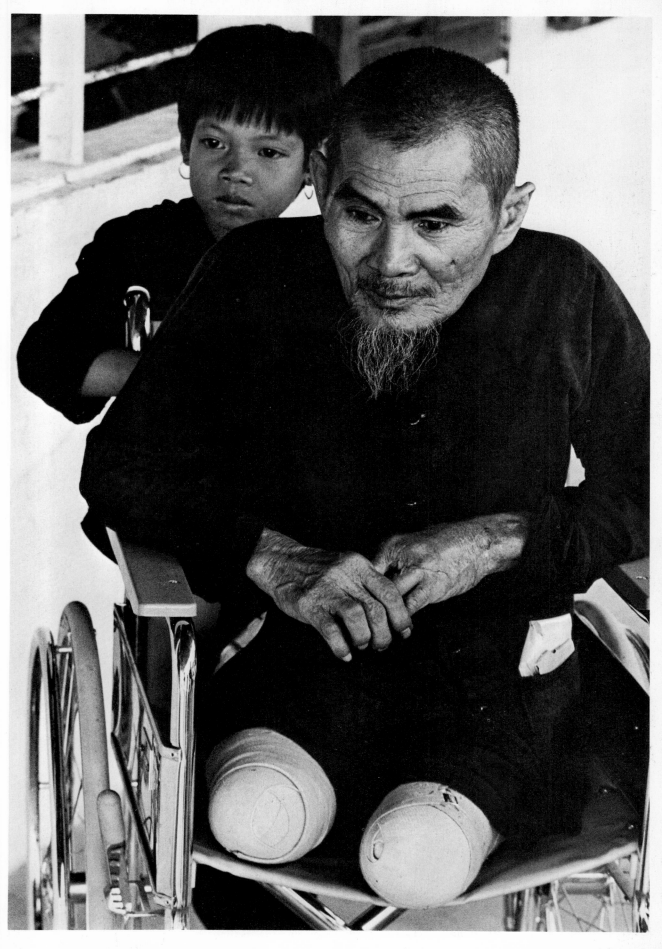

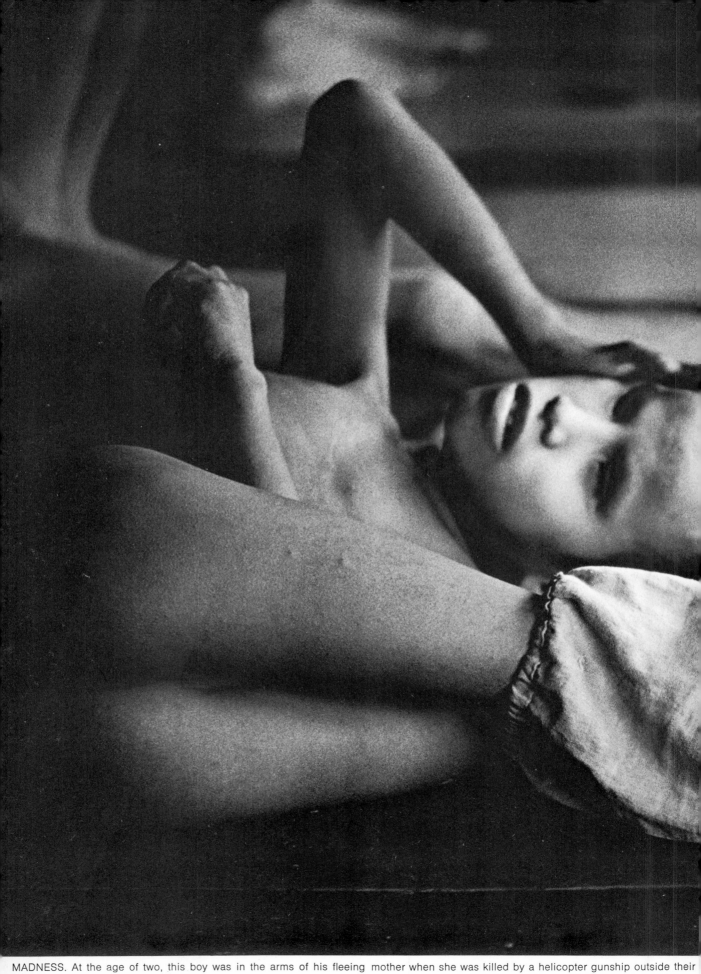

MADNESS. At the age of two, this boy was in the arms of his fleeing mother when she was killed by a helicopter gunship outside their

urvived but went insane. Now he spends his life chained up. When helicopters pass overhead he goes berserk trying to shut out their soun

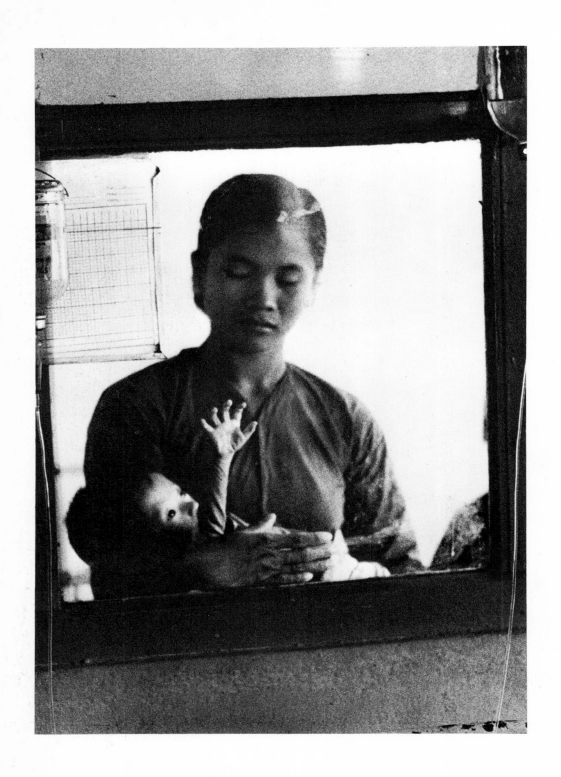

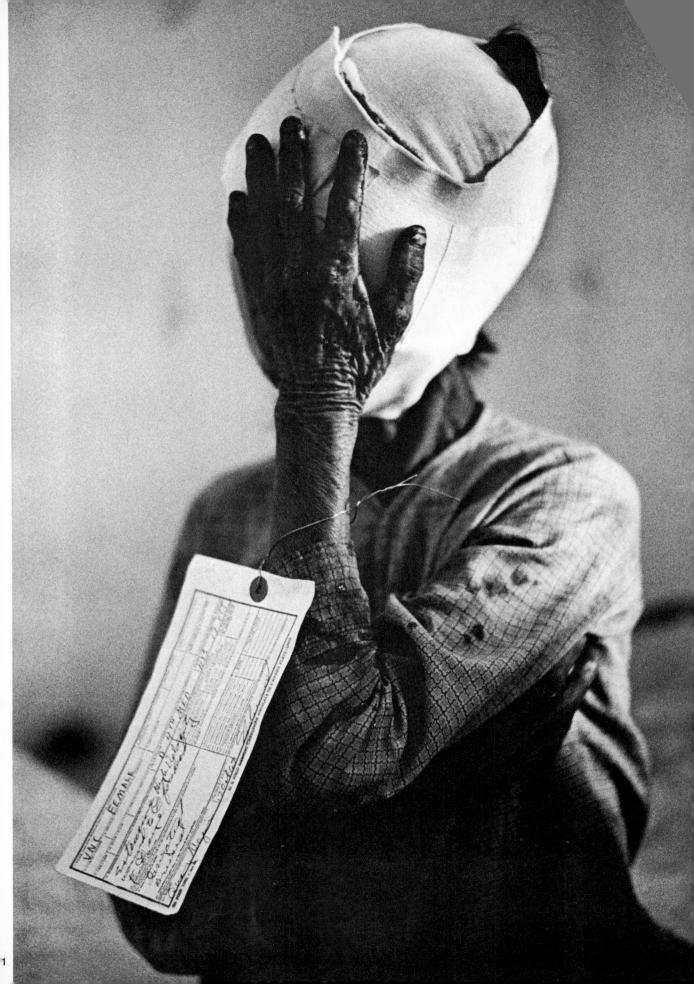

Christmas 1970 — New Year's 1971

HOLIDAY GREETINGS FROM CHAU DOC PROVINCE
REPUBLIC OF VIETNAM

As we phase out the Old Year and welcome the New Year, we do so with the confidence that what we Americans are fighting for in Vietnam is right — and that God has always been on the side of those who are right. The voices of dissension have risen many times throughout the land — but they have not spoken for the majority of the people — and they have not prevailed. We can look back with pride on another year of slow but steady progress in the long struggle we and our Vietnamese allies have engaged in to bring a just and honorable peace to this land.

And looking back over the sacrifices that so many Americans have made here — sacrifies that I have personally observed in my five years in Vietnam — I am even more proud to say — I am an American. And I believe that we must rededicate ourselves to the effort that will bring the final victory and ask ourselves — what is it about this great country of ours — these United States of America — that has inspired brave men to fight and die for her for so many years in order to preserve her freedom.

And I have chosen these words which I hope will mean as much to you as they have to me for so many years —

I AM THE NATION

I am the nation. I was born on the Fourth of July, 1776, and the Declaration of Independence is my birth certificate. The bloodlines of the world run in my veins, because I offered freedom to the oppressed. I am many things and many people. I am the nation.

I am 200 million living souls — and the ghost of millions who have lived and died for me.

I am Nathan Hale and Paul Revere. I stood at Lexington and fired the shot heard round the world. I am Washington, Jefferson and Patrick Henry. I am John Paul Jones, the Green Mountain Boys and Davey Crockett. I am Lee and Grant and Abe Lincoln.

I remember the Alamo, the Maine and Pearl Harbor. When freedom called I answered and stayed until it was over, over there. I left my heroic dead in Flanders Fields, on the rock of Corregidor, on the bleak slopes of Korea and in the steaming jungle of Vietnam.

I am the Brooklyn Bridge, the wheat lands of Kansas and the granite hills of Vermont. I am the coal fields of the Virginias and Pennsylvania, the fertile lands of the west, the Golden Gate and Grand Canyon. I am Independence Hall, the *Monitor* and the *Merrimac.*

I am big. I sprawl from the Atlantic to the Pacific . . . my arms reach out to embrace Alaska and Hawaii . . . three million square miles throbbing with industry. I am more than five million farms. I am forest, field, mountain and desert. I am quiet villages . . . and cities that never sleep.

You can look at me and see Ben Franklin walking down the streets of Philadelphia with his breadloaf under his arm. You can see the lights of Christmas, and hear the strains of "Auld Lang Syne" as the calendar turns.

I am Babe Ruth and the World Series. I am 130,000 schools and colleges and 320,000 churches where my people worship God as they think best. I am a ballot dropped in a box, the roar of a crowd in a stadium and the voice of a choir in a cathedral. I am an editorial in a newspaper and a letter to a Congressman.

I am Eli Whitney and Stephen Foster. I am Tom Edison, Albert Einstein and Billy Graham. I am Horace Greeley, Will Rogers and the Wright Brothers. I am George Washington Carver, Daniel Webster and Jonas Salk.

I am Longfellow, Harriet Beecher Stowe, Walt Whitman and Jonas Salk.

Yes, I am the Nation, and these are the things that I am. I was conceived in freedom and God willing, in freedom I will spend the rest of my days.

May I possess always — the integrity, the courage and the strength to keep myself unshackled, to remain a citadel of freedom and a beacon of hope to the world.

And although Plato once said — "Only the dead have seen the end of war"—it is my hope, that with God's help, on some future Christmas or New Year in the long roll call of unborn generations, Americans may awaken to a world of total peace. Until it does, we must maintain our strength, defend our rights, and fight, if need be, to preserve our freedom.

We of MACCORDS Advisory Team 64, Chau Doc, Vietnam, here on the Cambodian border are wholly dedicated to helping the Vietnamese help themselves and in so doing are helping to keep our great country free.

Please accept my sincere wish that the coming Christmas Season and the New Year will bring a full measure of happiness to you and your loved ones.

JOHN VIRGIL SWANGO
Province Senior Advisor
Chau Doc Province

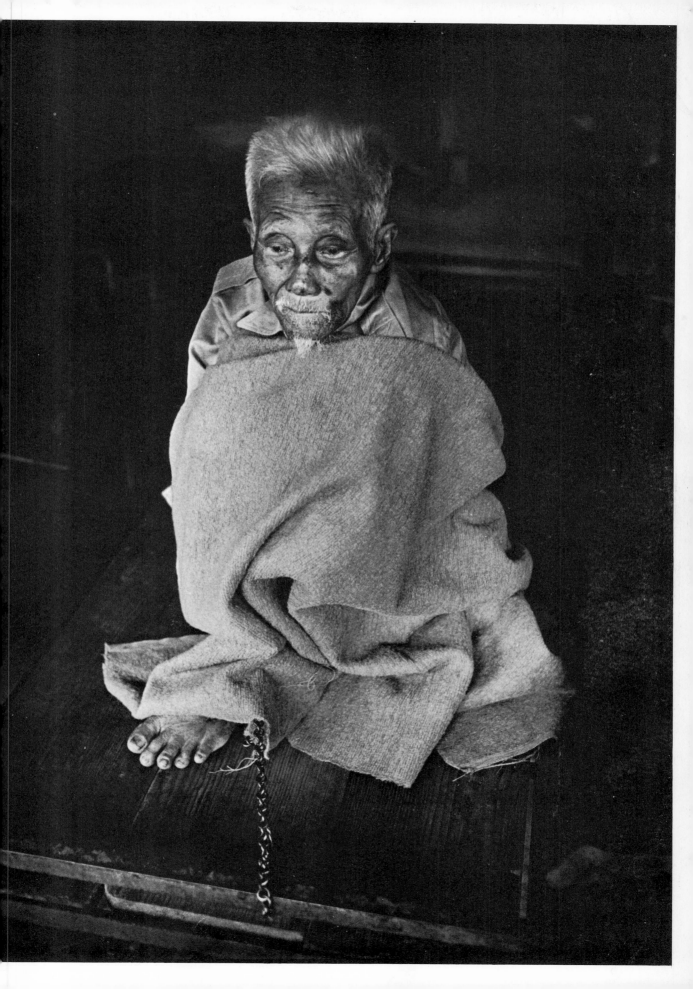

" 'We are here to ensure freedom for the Vietnamese to choose the kind of government they want' . . . is as implausible as Bell Telephone saying it believes everyone should have the freedom to choose which phone company to patronize."

"Amidst all the rhetoric about 'saving Vietnam from the Communists' one fact is always conveniently forgotten . . . that Vietnam once had a Communist government. Furthermore, the people chose it—on January 6, 1946, during the first election ever allowed to the Vietnamese. . . . It is obvious that this one fact completely negates America's stated purpose for being in Vietnam, because America can hardly claim to be helping the Vietnamese choose the kind of government they want when they made their choice years ago."

PHILIP JONES GRIFFITHS is a Welshman who has spent three years covering the Vietnam war as a Magnum photographer. His pictures have appeared internationally in leading magazines. It is the author's contention that the war's metamorphosis from a ground-troop operation to a fully automated, and impersonal death-dealing technology is enabling the United States to bring home the troops and continue the war without them.

COLLIER BOOKS
866 THIRD AVENUE, NEW YORK, N.Y. 10022

055410